CHILDREN, PARENTS
AND THE LAW

CHILDREN, PARENTS AND THE LAW

a Consumer Publication

Consumers' Association
publishers of **Which?**
14 Buckingham Street
London WC2N 6DS

a Consumer Publication

edited by   Edith Rudinger

published by   Consumers' Association
publishers of **Which?**

illustrations by   Jo Bampton

© Consumers' Association November 1985

ISBN 0 340 37256 7
0 85202 301 4

Photoset by Paston Press, Norwich
Printed in England by Page Bros (Norwich) Ltd

contents

Throughout this book

for 'he' read 'he or she'

foreword

Despite dozens of statutes and countless regulations, much of the law concerning the rights and status of children and their parents (or parents and their children) is incomplete, unspecific on many points, and has some grey areas. The need for clarification and consolidation is evident from the number of Law Commission reports and working papers on family law and children that have been produced recently (and are still to come). These generally summarise the need for reform, with recommendations where and how this reform may be achieved. In the meantime, this book sets out the situation under the existing laws, about what parents can and what they must do in relation to their children's upbringing and wellbeing. It explains when children themselves can make choices, are expected to take over responsibility for their own actions and can enforce their rights. Children are not a problem group, but when things go wrong the state or the local authority can intervene on behalf of the child or the parent.

No attempt is made in the book to deal with the emotional or psychological aspects of family relationships, but sources of advice and help are given, including the many voluntary organisations and support groups that now exist.

Throughout this book

for 'he' read 'he or she'

when a child is born

The birth of a child gives rise to a number of obligations on the part of the parents and the state.

registering the birth

The birth of every child born in this country must be registered within 42 days of the baby's birth (in Scotland, 21 days).

Where the parents are married, it is normally the father or mother who is required to provide particulars to the registrar of births for the sub-district where the birth took place.

If, for any reason, neither the father nor mother is able to register the birth, the birth must be registered by another 'qualified informant': for example, a person who was present at the birth of the child or the occupier of the house or other premises where the birth took place.

The sub-district offices of the registrar of births and deaths are listed in the telephone directory. If you are unsure which is the sub-district where the birth took place, check at the post office or library.

If your child is born in hospital, the local registrar may have an arrangement with the hospital to come in on certain days to register births which have taken place there.

If, before registering the birth, you leave the district where the baby was born, you need not go back in person to that district registrar. You can go to any registrar and give the particulars for him to complete a form of declaration about the birth. You and the registrar sign this declaration which he sends to the registrar of the sub-district where the birth took place.

The prescribed particulars which are entered in the register include: when and where the birth took place, the names and sex of the child, details of the mother and father. If the parents are married to each other, the registrar will want to know the name, birthplace and occupation of the father (no proof of this will be required).

The name and surname of the mother have to be given as they were at the time of the birth, as well as her maiden surname and, if different, the surname in which she married the child's father. From 1 January 1986, the occupation of the mother may also be entered.

choice of child's name

The registrar will ask in what surname or family name the child is to be brought up. This does not need to be the surname used by either the father or the mother but it is customary for a legitimate child or the child of a cohabiting couple to take the surname or family name of the father.

Parents generally choose the child's forename(s) when registering the birth, and the name(s) may be confirmed later by a religious baptism.

If no forenames have been chosen at the time of the registration, the child can still be registered, showing just the surname. The law allows for names given to a child within 12 months after the registration of the birth, whether in baptism or not, to be recorded in the birth entry. This applies if no forenames have been entered for the child at the time of registering or the forenames given subsequently are different from the names originally entered.

There is no law against using different surnames at different times and for different circumstances. Anyone can change his or her surname at any time without formality – by starting to use another name.

In Scotland, the formalities for registering the birth of a child are contained in the Registration of Births, Deaths and Marriages (Scotland) Act 1965. This Act provides that registration should be carried out by the parent or parents, or any relative of either having knowledge of the birth, or the occupier of the premises in which the birth took place, or any person present at the birth or having charge of the child. Whoever does the registering, must within 21 days attend personally at the local registrar's office to give information of statutory particulars regarding the birth.

illegitimate child
If the parents are not married to each other, the father is under no obligation to register the birth.

The mother of an illegitimate child does not need to give details of the father if she does not wish to: the part of the register giving particulars of the father may be left blank. Particulars of the father of an illegitimate child may, however, be entered

○ at the joint request of the mother and the father (in which case both sign the register)

○ at the sole request of the mother provided she can produce for the registrar a statutory declaration, signed by the father and witnessed by a solicitor, acknowledging paternity (in which case the father need not attend to sign the register)

○ where the mother has an affiliation order against the child's father (that is a court order which states that he is the child's father and requires him to pay maintenance).

The father of an illegitimate child has no independent right to have his name placed on the register.

Entry of the father's name on the register constitutes evidence of paternity for the purposes of subsequent affiliation proceedings, and could also constitute evidence of adultery if the mother or father was married to someone else at the time.

The mother can give the child any forenames and surname she chooses (even the father's without his consent).

– changing the entry

Details of the registration can be changed later in certain circumstances. For example, if the child is illegitimate and the father's name was not originally entered, the birth may subsequently be re-registered to include his name, at the joint request of the parents or on production of a statutory declaration by the father, or a copy of an affiliation order.

If the mother and father subsequently marry, the parents can apply within three months of their marriage to have the child's birth re-registered as legitimate. Application should be made to the Registrar General through the registrar of the district in which the child was born, using form LA1, which any registrar can provide. The original birth certificate of the child and a copy of the parents' marriage certificate should be sent with form LA1.

When re-registration has been authorised, one of the parents has to go to the registrar of the district where the child was born, or make a declaration of the required particulars before some other registrar. A note is made against the original entry, referring to the later one, and copies of the first entry are no longer issued unless a special application is made to the Registrar General for his authority to do so.

birth certificates

There is no fee for registering a birth and you will receive free a shortened form of the entry in the register – the birth certificate – at the time of registration. This certificate merely records the names, sex, date and place of birth of the child but not the parents' names and does not therefore disclose whether the child is illegitimate (or adopted). The birth certificate may be needed at later stages of life as proof of age or of place of birth.

A long form of birth certificate (a full copy of the entry which discloses details of parentage) and further 'short' certificates can be bought from the district registrar and, after a year or more, from the General Register Office, St Catherines House, 10 Kingsway, London WC2B 6JP; in Northern Ireland, from the

General Register Office, Oxford House, 49–55 Chichester Street, Belfast BT1 4HL; in Scotland, from the General Register Office for Scotland, New Register House, Edinburgh EH1 3YT.

getting on a doctor's list

When you register the birth, you will be given a pink card (form FP58), on which to apply for the child to be taken on by an NHS general practitioner.

You are entitled to register your child with a local GP on the national health service panel. If you are uncertain or have any difficulties – for example, the doctor of your choice will not accept your child as a patient (perhaps his list of patients is already too large) – you should contact your local Family Practitioner Committee (Health Board, in Scotland). The address is in the telephone directory or obtainable from the local library or post office or citizens advice bureau.

After you have registered the child with a doctor, the Family Practitioner Committee will issue you with an NHS medical card, which gives the child's NHS number. Make sure you keep this in a safe place.

maternity rights and payments

The mother is entitled to a maternity grant from the state, not dependent on any national insurance contributions, provided she has lived in Great Britain for at least 26 weeks in the year up to the baby's birth. The grant must be claimed before the end of the third month from the baby's birth.

She is also entitled to a maternity allowance based on her own national insurance contributions. This is payable for 18 weeks provided she applies within the 3 weeks after the beginning of the 14th week before the week in which the birth is due – otherwise she may not receive the allowance for the full 18-week period.

DHSS leaflet N1 17A gives full details of maternity grant and maternity allowance. Neither of these payments is taxable.

A woman who was employed before the birth of her child and has met the statutory condition for the right to return to her former (or an equivalent) job before the end of the 29th week from the birth of the baby, must give 21 days' notice of her intention to return. The Department of Employment's booklet *Employment rights for the expectant mother* (No 4 in the employment legislation series) gives full details.

There are a number of payments and concessions from the state that a mother and/or child may be entitled to. The DHSS issues a summarising leaflet FB2 *Which benefit?* and current rates are given in leaflet N1 196, available from social security offices. There are also DHSS leaflets FB8 *Babies and benefits*, MV11 *Free milk and vitamins*.

domicile

Every person has a 'domicile'. Domicile is a legal concept, not necessarily related to residence, however long such residence may have lasted. Essentially, it is the country which one regards to be home and, if not living there, to which one will return in the end. Nationality and domicile are not the same thing.

Domicile of origin is not determined by the place where a child is born but is the domicile of the child's father (mother if illegitimate) at the date of the child's birth. The domicile of a child while under the age of 16 remains that of the parent. Once over the age of 16, the child can acquire a different 'domicile of choice'. No one can have more than one domicile at any one time.

The law of your domicile is the law that you are subject to. For example, if you are domiciled in England, the law of that jurisdiction applies; if in Scotland, you come under scottish jurisdiction. Domicile affects, amongst other things, under which law of the land you can marry – or divorce.

nationality and passport

A child born now in the UK is automatically a british citizen provided that at the time of the birth one or both of the parents is a british citizen or is settled in the UK. If a parent is a national of another country, the child may hold dual citizenship, which is permitted by some countries, including the UK.

If the child is illegitimate, only the mother's nationality or settled status is relevant.

For a child not born a british citizen, there are provisions for applying for the registration of minors as british citizens.

Enquiries should be addressed to the Home Office Nationality Division, Lunar House, 90 Wellesley Road, Croydon, Surrey CR9 2BY.

– passports

Parents can include children on either parent's passport while the child is under 16. The child can then travel abroad only with that parent. A legitimate child can be included on both parents' passports and can then travel abroad with either parent. An illegitimate child can be on the mother's passport only.

A child may have a standard passport in his or her own name at any age but needs a parent's consent on the application form while under the age of 18. A child may not hold a british visitor's passport until he is 8 years old and until the age of 18 needs a parent's consent on the application form for one.

parental rights and duties

The law provides little guidance on what parents must or can do with their children while a child is under 18 – the age of majority. The law is a little clearer about what parents should not or must not do, and steps in mainly when things go wrong. Such controls as there are reduce considerably after a child passes compulsory school age, and cease completely on a child's marriage, at whatever age.

who has parental rights?

All legal rights and duties in respect of legitimate children under the age of majority used to be vested in the father to the total exclusion of the mother. The position now is that both parents have equal rights, which each may exercise separately. If husband and wife have some profound disagreement on any question affecting a child's welfare, they may apply to the court (High Court, county court or magistrates' court) for a decision, and the court may make an order. In resolving such disputes between parents, the court has to regard the child's welfare as the 'first and paramount consideration' and will treat the rights and authority of the mother and the father as being equal.

If the parents subsequently separate but do not divorce, the position goes on exactly as before, with both parents retaining equal rights unless any court orders are made. Where the parents divorce, the divorce court has to agree the allocation of parental rights and duties between the parents, making the necessary orders about who has custody of the children, who has their care and control and about access to the other parent.

A step-parent has no legal status but assumes certain responsibilities by treating a stepchild as a member of the family.

If one parent dies, all parental rights and duties vest in the surviving parent unless a guardian has been appointed to act jointly with the surviving parent. If a child under the age of 17 has been orphaned and no guardian has been appointed, the local authority is under a duty to receive him into their care if they consider this to be 'necessary in the interests of the welfare of the child'.

Adoption has the effect of vesting all parental rights and duties in the adoptive parents to the exclusion of the natural parents.

With an illegitimate child, all parental rights and duties vest exclusively in the mother. The only way in which the father can obtain any rights with regard to the child is by applying to the court for custody or access; such an order is only effective while the mother and father are not living together.

what parental rights?

Over the years, parental 'rights' have been replaced by responsibilities. Lord Denning, when he was Master of the Rolls, said "the legal right of the parent to custody of a child is a dwindling right, which the courts hesitate to enforce against the wishes of the child, the older he is. It starts with the right of control and ends with little more than advice".

If there is a dispute before the court concerning the welfare of a child, it will consider that the child's interests are of paramount importance. This may even result in a court refusing to enforce the parents' right to the custody of their child.

child leaving home
If your child has reached the age of, say, 16 and wants to leave home, perhaps to live with someone whom you consider to be undesirable, you would probably not be entitled to stop him

physically – and would probably commit an offence if you tried to do so. (The Court of Appeal has held that a parent can be guilty of 'false imprisonment' where the parent's restraint of a child's freedom of movement is an unreasonable exercise of parental rights.) You could, however, either have the child made a ward of court or ask the local authority to bring care proceedings on the grounds that the child is 'in moral danger' or is 'beyond parental control' (the local authority can only bring proceedings if the child is under 17).

If some person who has no parental rights takes your child from you, you will almost certainly be within your rights to take your child back without recourse to the courts at all. But where the child is being forcibly detained, you can apply to the court for the child to be made a ward of court. Or you can apply for a writ of *habeas corpus* for the child to be released to the court.

abduction

The common law offence of kidnapping arises if a child is taken by anyone against the child's will or when he is too young for his consent to be valid and when a parent takes away a child over the age of 14 using force or fraud.

It is also an offence for anyone acting without lawful authority or excuse to take a girl under the age of 16 out of the possession of her parents or other persons having lawful care of her, against their will. Neither force nor fraud needs to have been used: mere persuasion to leave home is sufficient for it to be an offence.

The Child Abduction Act 1984 does away with the need to show force or fraud where a child under the age of 16 has been abducted. The Act penalises a person not connected with a child who, without lawful authority or reasonable excuse, removes the child from, or keeps the child out of, the lawful control of anyone entitled to it. (But it is a defence for the accused person to show that he believed that the abducted child was aged 16 or over or, where the child is illegitimate, that he had reasonable grounds for believing himself to be the child's father.)

Where the parents are separated or divorced and the parent with whom the child does not normally live takes the child away, the other parent would be entitled to apply to the court for an order that the child be returned immediately. Where there is a custody order, the snatching parent could, in theory, be committed to prison for contempt of court.

– out of the country

The Child Abduction Act confers a power of arrest without warrant so that the police are able to take effective enforcement action against a person whom they reasonably suspect of attempting illegally to remove a child abroad.

Where there appears to be a real and imminent danger of a child's illegal removal abroad, the Home Office can be asked to take whatever action is possible at ports and airports to try to prevent this. The Home Office can be contacted by telephone during normal office hours on 01-213 3102 or 5185 for a port alert to be instituted.

If either parent or guardian or anyone else who has been awarded custody by a court order takes the child out of the UK without the appropriate consent of the other parent or the court, he or she will have committed a criminal offence for which he or she may be prosecuted.

There is at present no power to extract a child from a foreign country other than by the aggrieved parent taking the matter to the courts in that country – which is likely to be complicated, long-drawn out and expensive. The Foreign and Commonwealth Office Consular Department, Clive House, Petty France, London SW1H 9HD, can give some advice and assistance to UK parents whose children have been abducted abroad. There is also the Children Abroad Self-Help Group, Keighley Gingerbread Advice Centre, 33 Barlow Road, Keighley BD21 2EU.

The Child Abduction and Custody Act 1985, due to be brought into force in the first half of 1986, will enable the UK to ratify two international conventions relating to the return of children wrongfully removed from the country where they are habitually resident and to the recognition and enforcement of child custody decisions (including those relating solely to access) which have been made in their favour in another country. These conventions, when implemented, should help towards providing a solution to the problem of international child kidnapping.

control and discipline

The 'right' to control and discipline your children is based more on moral and social pressures than on the law.

The parent has the right to administer reasonable discipline including reasonable corporal punishment – subject to criminal sanctions for assault, or causing bodily harm, or cruelty to someone under 16. If a child has been persistently ill-treated, the local authority social services department might step in and take care proceedings.

Where a child is proving particularly troublesome, you can ask the local authority social worker for help and advice. In an extreme case, the local authority might bring care proceedings on the ground that the child is 'beyond parental control'.

Before taking extreme steps in such difficulties, parents should seek advice and counselling for themselves, the child and the whole family. The first point of contact for most parents is likely to be their GP, the health visitor or the local authority's social services department or child and family guidance centre.

Organisations that may be able to help – not least by showing parents that they are not unique in their fear that their feelings of frustration might lead to non-accidental injury to the child – include

Organisations for Parents under Stress (OPUS) (106 Godstone Road, Whyteleafe, Surrey CR3 0EB, telephone: 01-645 0469, 24-hour crisis number: 01-645 0505)
is a co-ordinating body for support groups such as 'Parents anonymous', 'Parents lifeline', 'Parents helpline', with a network of telephone contacts answered by parent volunteers who are trained to provide support to parents in distress.

The British Association for Counselling (37a Sheep Street, Rugby, Warwickshire CV21 3BX, telephone: 0788-78328)
can put people who feel in need of counselling in touch with a counselling service or with individual counsellors who are members of the association.

Family Network (organised by the National Children's Home, 85 Highbury Park, London N5 1UD, telephone: 01-226 2033)
is a network of telephone helplines providing a listening and advice service supported by social work help and local information, primarily intended for people who need support urgently at a time of crisis. There are twelve network telephone numbers obtainable from the Manchester network number: 061-236 9873.

Exploring Parenthood (39–41 North Road, London N7 9DP, telephone: 01-607 9647)
runs workshops for parents with the aim of preventing minor anxieties becoming major problems.

– for the child

A teenage, or even younger, child may come to feel so out of tune with his parents, or so misused by one or other of them, that he needs to seek advice and help from an outside, impartial, source. There are a number of groups who offer counselling and assistance to children who are at variance with their parents and/or want to get away from home. Some are locally based and the nearest citizens advice bureau would know of them; some deal with specific situations, such as homelessness, others are regional centres of a national network.

The **National Association of Young People's Counselling and Advisory Services** (headquarters: 17–23 Albion Street, Leicester LE1 6GD, telephone: 0533 554775)
is the co-ordinating body for some 80 regional centres giving advice to young people on any topic, including legal.

The **National Children's Bureau** (8 Wakley Street, London EC1V 7QE, telephone: 01-278 9441)
is an independent membership organisation to promote and safeguard the best interests of children. It is not able to provide advice or counselling on individual problems, but offers lists of organisations concerned with the problems of young people and various aspects of parent/child/family/community relationships, in categories such as juvenile crime and delinquency, education, adoption and foster care, children's rights, care and development of children, abuse and neglect, families with young children; also bibliographies in similar categories.

leaving a child with other people

There is no law making it an offence to leave children under a certain age on their own. The one specific situation covered by the law is the requirement that anyone in charge of a child under the age of 12 must take reasonable precautions to prevent the child from burning or scalding.

What is an offence, however, is for anyone over the age of 16 who is in charge of a child under that age to be 'cruel' to that child. This can include neglect and exposure to unnecessary suffering – such as leaving a small child unattended in a car – as well as actual ill treatment. The child's age is a crucial factor: a 14-year-old can be expected to be able to take better care of himself on his own than a 4-year-old.

Anyone who looks after someone else's child (if not related to that child) under the age of five for more than 2 hours a day and is paid for this in cash or kind must be registered with the local authority's social services department as a childminder. The local authority can impose requirements on registered childminders, such as restricting the number of children to be looked after on the premises, and checks on the suitability of the premises with regard to space, safety and cleanliness.

The **National Childminding Association** (204–206 High Street, Bromley, Kent BR1 1PP, telephone: 01-464 6164) has a booklet *I need a childminder* (20p) giving information to parents who want their child to be looked after by a childminder.

child's religion

Parents are entitled to choose the religion in which their child is brought up. At any age, the child can choose to join a different religious group, whether the parents acquiesce or not, so long as the new religious authority accepts him.

medical treatment

Although it is unusual, it is not unlawful for a child of any age to register with a general practitioner who is not the parent's doctor. The parents have to do the original registering so, in practice, the parents choose the child's first doctor. The child can go and see the doctor without the parents' consent. Any duty the doctor has to consult the child's parents applies whether or not the doctor is the parents' general practitioner.

A recent decision in the Court of Appeal held that doctors and family planning clinics may not advise on or prescribe contraceptives to girls under 16 without their parents' permission. But the House of Lords has now reversed this.

− surgery

While the child is under 16, the parent or guardian has to sign the consent form for surgical treatment. In Scotland consent may be given by a boy over the age of fourteen, a girl over the age of twelve; it is medical practice, however, for the parents to be consulted where the child is under sixteen.

If the child needs an operation or treatment in an emergency, it is the doctor's duty to do what he or she thinks is in the patient's interests, even if the parents do not consent. In less extreme cases, the doctor may refer the matter to the local authority who may take proceedings to have the child made a ward of court. The court will then make the decision and order whatever it regards to be in the best interests of the child.

Anyone who is concerned about the child's medical treatment or lack of it and can show sufficient right to intervene can apply to the High Court to have a child made a ward of court.

− dental treatment

There is no requirement for a child (or anyone) to be registered with any particular dentist. Dental treatment on the NHS is free of charge until the child reaches the age of 18 (or 19 if still a full-time student), but while the child is under 16, the parent or guardian has to sign the dentist's NHS treatment form.

Once over the age of 16, a child who requires dentures will only be entitled to these free of charge if still at school or a full-time student and under the age of 19.

Once a child reaches the age of 16, he may go to a dentist for treatment without needing a parent's signature, and can sign – or refuse to sign – his own consent form for surgery.

– in hospital
When a child is in hospital, one or both parents should be allowed to be with the child for as much of the time as they choose and the child's condition allows. DHSS guidelines for the care of children in hospital include that children should not be put in wards for adults and should be in the care of specially trained staff, that parents should be able to visit at any time and to stay overnight if they wish. But parents may need to be persistent to achieve these facilities.

The **National Association for the Welfare of Children in Hospital (NAWCH)** (Argyle House, 29–31 Euston Road, London NW1 2SD, telephone: 01-833 2041)
exists to help parents before, during and after their child's stay in hospital, and can give direct help and advice; there are over 70 local branches. Publications available from NAWCH include a booklet *Children in hospital: an action guide for parents* (£1).

vaccination
The DHSS recommends a schedule for vaccinating children against certain diseases at certain ages but parents are not obliged to have their children vaccinated and cannot be penalised for not doing so. The DHSS recommended timetable is

in the first year

3 to 6 months:	4 to 6 months:	6 to 8 weeks later:
1st dose of triple vaccine (diphtheria, tetanus and whooping cough) or of double (diphtheria and tetanus) and oral polio vaccine	2nd dose of triple (or double) and polio vaccines	3rd dose of triple (or double) and polio vaccines

in the second year
measles
(not within 3 weeks of any other vaccination)

on starting school
diphtheria, tetanus and polio boosters

10 to 13 years:
tuberculosis   girls only:
(BCG vaccination is given   German measles (rubella)
only if a skin-test shows child
is not immune to tuberculosis)

15 to 19 years or on leaving school
polio and tetanus boosters

A report in *Which?* July 1982 on vaccination discusses the
effectiveness and contra-indications. There is a Health
Education Council booklet on immunisation against the five
dangerous diseases, available free in clinics and surgeries.

prescriptions
A woman who has had a baby does not have to pay NHS
prescription charges for 12 months from the birth. If she did
not get an exemption certificate while she was pregnant,
form A (*Free prescriptions*) on DHSS leaflet P11 should now be
completed.

While a child is under 16, he is automatically entitled free of
charge to medicines prescribed under the NHS. All the parent
needs to do is to sign the appropriate declaration on the
prescription form. Once the child reaches 16, he can apply for
exemption on the ground of his low income, for example, if he
is still at school or a student; he remains entitled if the family
is getting FIS or supplementary benefit. (See DHSS leaflet P11 *NHS
prescriptions – how to get them free.*)

There is no charge for sight tests under the NHS; children under
the age of 16 (or up to 19 if still in full-time education) can get
glasses free in the children's range of NHS lenses and frames. If
a child between the ages of 10 and 16 (or a student up to age
19) wants frames from the adults' range, he can pay for these
and get the lenses free. For further information, see DHSS leaflet
G11 *NHS glasses.*

marriage of a child under 18

No one under the age of 16 can validly marry in this country (such a marriage would be void).

If a child is 16 or 17 (except in Scotland), the written consent of both parents is required if they are both alive and living together. If one parent is dead, consent is required from the surviving parent and any jointly acting guardian. Where both parents are dead, consent is required from any guardians appointed by the parents or the court. Where no guardian was appointed in such circumstances, no consent is necessary.

If the parents are divorced or separated, consent is required from the parent to whom custody has been given. Where the child is illegitimate, consent is normally required from the mother only. Where a local authority has passed a 'parental rights resolution' under the Child Care Act 1980, the local authority's consent will be required. If a child has been made a ward of court, the consent of the court will be required.

The marriage of a young person between the ages of 16 and 18 is valid, however, even without parental consent.

Parental consent does not need to be given to a marriage which is preceded by publication of banns in church or chapel (but a parent may dissent when the banns are called, thus making the banns void, so that the marriage cannot take place). Nor does the rule apply in the event of a widow or widower under the age of 18 marrying again.

Parental consent may be dispensed with where the relevant person is inaccessible or is under any disability, in which case the court can be asked to make an order dispensing with consent.

Where the parent or guardian refuses to give consent, the couple can apply to the court (generally the magistrates' court) which may decide to give an over-ruling consent.

who cannot marry whom

a man must not marry

mother
adoptive mother
former adoptive mother
daughter
adoptive daughter
former adoptive daughter
father's mother
mother's mother
son's daughter
daughter's daughter
sister
wife's mother
wife's daughter
father's wife
son's wife
father's father's wife
mother's father's wife
wife's father's mother
wife's mother's mother
wife's son's daughter
wife's daughter's daughter
son's son's wife
daughter's son's wife
father's sister
mother's sister
brother's daughter
sister's daughter

a woman must not marry

father
adoptive father
former adoptive father
son
adoptive son
former adoptive son
father's father
mother's father
son's son
daughter's son
brother
husband's father
husband's son
mother's husband
daughter's husband
father's mother's husband
mother's mother's husband
husband's father's father
husband's mother's father
husband's son's son
husband's daughter's son
son's daughter's husband
daughter's daughter's husband
father's brother
mother's brother
brother's son
sister's son

Any such marriage would be void.

duty to maintain

The law makes a basic assumption that it is the parents' duty to maintain and to provide accommodation for their children. It will intervene only where something has gone wrong.

It is an offence for any person who has the custody, charge or care of any child under the age of 16 wilfully to neglect, abandon or expose the child in a manner likely to cause unnecessary suffering or injury to health. A parent or other person will be deemed to have neglected a child if he or she fails to provide adequate food, clothing, medical aid or lodging for the child.

The law leaves it to the parents to devote such part of their resources as they see fit to the welfare of their children. There is no procedure under which, for example, an older child can take proceedings against his parents if they are wealthy but refuse to devote any money to his education. Once a child has reached the age of 18, parents are under no obligation to maintain the child at all, or to provide accommodation for him – although moral and social pressures to do so are usually strong.

– through the court
Where there is a breakdown in the parents' relationship, however, the position is rather different. In proceedings in the county court for divorce, nullity, judicial separation, or for financial orders in a magistrates' court, the court has wide powers to order either husband or wife to make financial provision for any child who is a 'child of the family'. The definition embraces natural children, children the couple have adopted, and also any other child who has been treated as a child of the family (other than one boarded out by a local authority or voluntary organisation).

A court order for a child's maintenance normally ceases when the child reaches the age of 17, but can continue so long as the child is receiving full-time education or training, or if there are special circumstances, such as the child being handicapped. The court can then, in theory, order maintenance for a child of the family up to any age – for instance, 22 for a child who is still studying at university.

Where there is a magistrates' court order for maintenance, the child himself may apply to the magistrates for a variation of the maintenance order once he has reached the age of 16.

The county court also has power to make orders for the maintenance of legitimate children in guardianship and in wardship proceedings, and when it directs that the child be placed in local authority care.

Where a husband and wife are separated and the DHSS are paying supplementary benefit to the mother, the DHSS may apply through the magistrates' court for an order that the father make an appropriate contribution. The Supplementary Benefits Act 1976 provides that a man and woman shall be liable to maintain their children, whether legitimate or illegitimate. Where the child is illegitimate, the DHSS may apply for an order against the father. The DHSS may also (but rarely does) bring criminal proceedings for failure to maintain.

children to parent
Parents used to be entitled to the domestic services of their children while under the age of majority, but there is no longer any means whereby this may be enforced.

There is no law entitling parents to demand money from their child towards the child's keep, even if he has started earning.

Once a child is 18, the position is entirely voluntary: the child is not obliged to pay any money but, conversely, the parents are not obliged to provide children with their keep or a roof over their head.

At the other end of the scale, an adult son or daughter who supports a mother or mother-in-law who is widowed, divorced or separated from her husband is entitled to a tax allowance provided the mother's or mother-in-law's income is no more than the amount of the basic state retirement pension for a single person.

child benefit

As soon as a child is born, the parent should claim child benefit, which is paid irrespective of income. This is a tax-free weekly amount (at present, £7 per child) which remains payable until the child reaches the age of 16.

A single parent is entitled to one parent benefit, an additional weekly payment (at present, £4.55 per week), irrespective of the number of children. One parent benefit can be claimed by any parent who is bringing up a child alone – a widowed parent, or a married parent as soon as divorce proceedings have started or after being separated for 13 weeks.

When the child leaves school, child benefit will continue to be payable until the first monday of September, January or after Easter following his last term at school (unless he gets a job or joins a youth training scheme (YTS) in the mean time).

Child benefit may continue to be paid until the child reaches the age of 19 while he is still in full-time education at school or college up to A-level standard, but not if studying for a degree or a diploma, a professional qualification or is training under the YTS.

You may only claim if the child is living with you or you are contributing at least £7 (at the present rate) a week towards his maintenance. This means that you may be able to claim even if you are not the child's natural parent.

You will not be disqualified if your child is at boarding school or is absent from you for short temporary periods but the right to claim will be lost if the child has been in local authority care for more than eight weeks (unless he is allowed home for at least one day per week).

The basic rule is that the person with whom the child lives has priority in claiming child benefit. Where the parents (married or unmarried) are living together, the mother has priority, unless she consents in writing to the father making the claim.

A claim should be made on form CH2 (available from local social security offices) or on the form sent with the maternity grant, accompanied by the child's birth certificate. There is a separate claim form (CH11A) for one parent benefit.

You will receive a book of orders which are cashable at the post office every four weeks. You may ask to have your benefit paid weekly if you are a single parent or are receiving family income supplement or supplementary benefit. You may ask, if you prefer, to have the payment made direct into a bank account or building society account.

For further information about child benefit see DHSS leaflets
CH1   *Child benefit*
CH4   *Child benefit for children away from home*
CH4A *Child benefit for children in the care of a local authority*
CH7   *Child benefit for children aged 16 or over*
CH11 *One parent benefit for people bringing up children alone.*

supplementary benefit

If you are in receipt of supplementary benefit (SB), the birth of a child will automatically increase your 'requirements' by (at the present rate) £10.10 a week (if you give birth to more than one child, you can claim £10.10 per child). You have to inform the DHSS of the child's birth and produce a birth certificate.

The child benefit you get is counted in with weekly income and will reduce your entitlement to supplementary benefit £ for £ – for example, if you get child benefit of £7 a week while in receipt of SB, your additional SB 'requirement' will be only £3.10 for that child. However, extra weekly payments may be claimed for regular special needs such as extra heating and, if you have a child under 5, extra laundry costs.

When you are on supplementary benefit, you may be entitled to claim a single lump sum payment for one-off expenses connected with the baby's needs – for example, baby clothing, nappies, cot, bedclothes for the cot, baby bath, carry cot or pram – and also for maternity clothes.

As a result of the birth of the child, you or your partner may now be eligible to claim supplementary benefit for the first time, provided that whichever of you is claiming does not have a full-time job (that is, works less than 30 hours per week).

Whether and how much SB you are entitled to depends on your income and assessed 'requirements' and any savings you have. DHSS leaflet SB1 (available at post offices as well as social security offices) gives basic details and includes a simple claim form, and leaflets SB8 and SB9 (from social security offices) tell you what happens when you have claimed.

Other relevant DHSS leaflets are
SB16 *Lump sum payments*
SB17 *Help with heating costs*
SB18 *The capital rule*
SB19 *Weekly payments for special needs*

family income supplement

A married or unmarried couple or a single parent with at least one child under the age of 16 (under 19 if still at school) may be entitled to claim family income supplement (FIS), provided the child is living at home or the claimant is contributing towards the child's maintenance and the family's weekly income falls short of the specified limit. In the case of a couple, either the man or the woman must be in paid work for at least 30 hours a week (24 hours in the case of a single parent). See DHSS leaflet N1 248 on ways of claiming for couples.

FIS is calculated by reference to a weekly income limit, set by the government. If your gross income is less than this, you will get FIS. The amount will be half the difference between your income and your FIS level. FIS is not taxable.

weekly income limit
The weekly income limits depend on the number of children in the family and their ages.

FIS *limit for 1 child*
£97.50 under 11
£98.50 aged 11 to 15
£99.50 aged 16 and over

for each additional child add
£11.50 if under 11
£12.50 if 11 to 15
£13.50 if 16 and over

Income is taken to be the family's gross weekly income before deductions for tax and national insurance, excluding

o child benefit and one parent benefit

o housing benefit

o children's income (other than maintenance received, for example, from divorced father).

If your resources are less than the weekly income limit, you will receive one half of the difference up to the maximum set by regulations. The current maxima are

age of children in family	*maximum* FIS *payment per week*
under 11	one child £25 *plus* £2.50 for each additional child under 11
aged 11 to 15	one child £25.50 *plus* £3 for each additional child between 11 and 15
aged 16 or over	one child £26 *plus* £3.50 for each additional child aged 16 or over

EXAMPLE
Family's total gross income is £95 a week. The wife has just had their first baby. FIS entitlement would be

$$\frac{97.50 - 95}{2} = \text{£1.25 per week}$$

If they already had a 6-year-old child, the FIS entitlement would be

$$\frac{109 - 95}{2} = \text{£7 per week}$$

If they already had a 12-year-old child and a 6-year-old, their weekly income limit would be £98.50 + £11.50 + £11.50 = £121.50 and the FIS entitlement would be

$$\frac{121.50 - 95}{2} = \text{£13.25 per week}$$

making the claim
You should claim as soon as possible because FIS cannot usually be back-dated to before the date of the claim.

A claim can be made on leaflet FIS1 (available from a post office or social security office) which requires detailed information. Send with the completed claim form your payslips for the requisite number of weeks.

If you qualify, you will receive FIS for 52 weeks from the date of the claim, in the form of weekly orders. FIS will continue to be payable for a year even if your circumstances change. You can renew the claim for subsequent years, at any time up to four weeks from the end of the current period.

Further information is in DHSS leaflets
FB4 *Help while you are working*
FB3 *Help for one parent families*

Anyone who is receiving supplementary benefit or family income supplement is entitled to a number of concessions, such as free school meals for the children.

in Scotland: parental rights and duties

In general, where there is a statutory provision affecting children in England and Wales, the same or an equivalent is to be found in Scotland. But there are exceptions, which are particularly important where matters of court procedure, wardship, criminal justice and social work provisions are concerned.

As in England, the law provides little guidance for parents but will intervene when the child is at risk, or affected by some change in family circumstances such as divorce.

Parental rights over a child in Scotland are traditionally seen in two distinct ways. Firstly, the right to guide and direct children under full age and control of their physical person, and, secondly, the right of legal administration, of managing the child's property and legal business or advising on such matters. In practice, both rights, or duties, normally fall on the parents but it is possible for the two roles to be quite distinct.

age of majority

Scottish law recognises two distinct stages in the capacity of children before they become adult. The first stage is known as pupillarity when a boy 'pupil' child is under the age of fourteen and a girl child is under the age of twelve.

The next stage is known as minority, when the minor can attain some contractual capacity and some independence of action. For instance, it is accepted that minor children in Scotland are capable of consenting to medical treatment notwithstanding the wishes of their parents. Similarly, a young person over the age of sixteen may marry without first obtaining parental consent. The age of minority subsists until the child attains eighteen years.

This age distinction has implications for criminal law also in that the abduction of a pupil child is regarded as theft in the law of Scotland, regardless of force or fraud, on the basis of the legal fiction which regards the pupil child as the property of the person having custody. Abduction of a minor, or even an adult, for any purpose is regarded as criminal whether or not force or fraud is used, the essential feature being the deprivation of personal freedom.

A parent in Scotland would be powerless to prevent a 16-year-old son or daughter from leaving the parental home.

duty to maintain
In Scotland the duty of a parent to maintain a child normally only has to be specified in connection with divorce proceedings. Orders made by the court to provide for custody and/or maintenance can be made only up to the 16th birthday of the child, not beyond. Once a child is sixteen, he or she has the right to raise a separate action for maintenance, or aliment as it is known in Scotland, in the sheriff court. It would be correct for a person over the age of sixteen but under the age of eighteen to have a curator *ad litem* acting on his or her behalf and named in the action but this is not always insisted upon and would not make the action invalid.

The obligation to maintain subsists until the child can, and does, maintain himself; if the child cannot, for reason of physical or mental incapacity or inability to obtain employment, the parents' obligation continues into adulthood. In practice, the courts are reluctant to make awards where the child has completed full-time education but the possibility does exist for, say, a student in Scotland to sue his parents for the parental contribution to his grant if that is not paid voluntarily. If the father and mother are dead, missing or poor, the duty to aliment passes to the grandparents.

A corresponding claim by parents to be alimented by their children does still exist under scottish law but such an action would be regarded as unusual except in special circumstances.

illegitimate children

In many respects, the illegitimate child is in no different a legal position from legitimate ones.

when is a child regarded as legitimate?

Children are legitimate when they are born or conceived while their parents are married to each other. If the parents marry after conception but before their child is born, he will be legitimate.

There is a presumption that all children born during a marriage are legitimate. (If the parties are separated under a decree of judicial separation, the presumption is the other way round.) If, therefore, a husband wishes to prove that he is not the father of a child born during the marriage, the burden is on him to prove that it is more probable than not that the child is not his. This could be done by means of blood tests or by showing that on the basis of the date he last had intercourse with his wife, he could not, or is unlikely to, be the father of the child. A child's legitimacy can be challenged and his illegitimacy proved at any time (for example, in a battle on succession rights to an estate).

If the parents of a child marry after he is born, the child will be legitimated as a result of the subsequent marriage provided the father's domicile at the time of the marriage is in this country. To all intents and purposes, the child will be in the same position as a legitimate child – for example, any reference in a will to 'legitimate children' includes such a child. Where, however, a right to inherit depends on the relative seniority of the children, the legitimated child ranks as if he had been born on the date of legitimation.

If the father's domicile is not in the UK at the time of marriage, the question whether the marriage legitimated the child depends upon the law of the country in which he was then domiciled.

A child may be legitimated by the subsequent marriage of his parents even if one or other of them was married to someone else at the time he was born.

> EXAMPLE
> H and W married in 1980. In February 1984, W commits adultery with X (domiciled in Wales) as a result of which a child (C) is born in October 1984. In January 1985, H commences divorce proceedings and a decree is made absolute in June 1985. On 6 August 1985, W and X marry: C is legitimated by their marriage from that date.

Some divorcing people are in a rush to get their decree absolute so that they can marry again before a child is born, not realising that if this cannot be done, their subsequent marriage will legitimate the child and the birth certificates can then be altered.

Children born during a marriage which is subsequently annulled will remain legitimate. In the case of a marriage that is void – for example, because it is bigamous – children born during such a 'marriage' will be legitimate if at the time of the marriage or of conception at least one of the parents reasonably believed the marriage to be in fact valid.

A child who was born illegitimate and is adopted is treated as the legitimate child of its adoptive parent(s).

the effect of illegitimacy

There are some differences in the status of the parents in relation to an illegitimate child compared to legitimate children. All parental rights rest solely with the mother to the exclusion of the father. If he is not living with the mother and the child, the only way in which the father may acquire any custody or access rights is by applying to the court under the Guardianship of Minors Act or by making the child a ward of court.

If the child is at any time going to be adopted by somebody else, the agreement of the father will not be required unless he has obtained an order for custody.

If an illegitimate child subsequently forms part of a married family, he will be a 'child of the family' for whom provision would have to be made in the context of divorce proceedings.

inheritance

On the death intestate (that is, without having made a will) of his father or mother, an illegitimate child is entitled to a share in the parent's estate in the same way as a legitimate child.

If a person who is illegitimate and has neither wife nor children dies intestate, his father and mother are entitled to inherit as if he had been legitimate. This, however, is as far as the inheritance provisions go: there is no further transmission up the line to grandparents or sideways to aunts or uncles.

Reference in a will or a trust deed to 'children' includes illegitimate children whether born before or after the date of the disposition unless the contrary intention is stated.

affiliation order

If the mother of an illegitimate child wants the father to contribute to the child's maintenance, she has to apply to the local magistrates' court for an affiliation order. But if the father brings up the child, he has no right to ask for maintenance from the mother.

The mother can apply provided she is a 'single woman' at the time of the application, or was single or separated at the date of the birth, or is divorced from the husband (who was not the father) she was married to at the time of the birth. She may qualify even if she has since married another man.

time limit for making the claim
Affiliation proceedings can be started even before the child is born, although the hearing will not take place until after the birth. The mother must start proceedings within three years of the birth.

She may, however, be allowed to claim later under certain circumstances, of which the following two are the most important:

○ She can claim at any time if the man alleged to be the father has paid money for the child's maintenance or made gifts of food or clothing at any time during the three years from the date of the child's birth. If they lived together in the same household with the father during this period, this of itself will be taken as proof that the father has paid maintenance.

○ She can claim within 12 months of the father's return to England or Wales if he had left the country within the three years after the date of the child's birth.

alternative claimant
If the mother does not apply and is receiving supplementary benefit, the DHSS may apply for an equivalent order under supplementary benefit law. They may do so even though the

woman cannot apply for an affiliation order because, for example, she has left her claim too late or she is not a 'single woman'. The DHSS's order is not an affiliation order as such, and would not continue to be in force if the mother ceases to be eligible for supplementary benefit. This is an important distinction for a mother to be aware of.

Similarly, if the child is in care, the local authority in whose care the child is have a right to bring affiliation proceedings.

going to the court

The mother has to go to the magistrates' court for the area in which she lives and fill in a 'complaint' form. A summons setting out the terms of the complaint will be sent by the court to the person she alleges is the father and he will be required to attend the hearing. Someone who is financially eligible can apply for legal aid for these proceedings.

At the hearing, the mother will have to satisfy the court that it is more probable than not that the person against whom she has brought proceedings is the father of the child. This has to be done even if the person named does not turn up (but the court will only proceed in his absence if they are satisfied that he has received a copy of the summons).

She will have to give evidence to prove the birth of her child and to show that the defendant is the father. Her evidence must be corroborated – that is, supported by other evidence. For example, a letter from the father admitting paternity, or a friend to whom he has made an admission, would be corroborative evidence, or his name appearing on the birth certificate.

The court has power to direct that blood tests should be made. While these can never show conclusively that a particular man is the father, they can show that a man could absolutely not be the father or that there is a degree of probability that he could be the father. If the court does direct that there shall be blood tests, blood samples will be taken from the mother, the child and the alleged father. No one can be forced to undergo a blood test, but if a person refuses, the court may draw certain inferences – for instance, if the mother refuses, that the man is not the father; if he refuses, that he is.

If the father does not contest the affiliation proceedings, it is generally possible for the mother to give formal evidence only and for maintenance payments then to be agreed.

If the mother succeeds in proving her case, the person against whom she made the claim will be adjudged to be the 'putative father' of the named child and the court order will state the amounts to be paid.

order for maintenance
The court may be asked to order that the father should pay

○ a lump sum, not exceeding £500. (This sum is usually for expenses incurred prior to the order; for example, the layette, clothes, pram)

and/or

○ periodical payments towards the maintenance of the child. (There is no upper limit for these.)

In deciding how much maintenance to order, the court will, amongst other factors, consider

○ the income, earning capacity, property and other financial resources which the mother of the child and the person adjudged to be the putative father of the child have or are likely to have in the foreseeable future

○ the financial needs, obligations and responsibilities which the mother and the putative father have or are likely to have in the foreseeable future

○ the financial needs of the child

○ the income, earning capacity (if any), property and other financial resources of the child

○ any physical or mental disability of the child.

Both parties will be asked to provide information about their income and outgoings and assets.

Periodical payments are usually ordered to be made weekly or monthly. If the mother applies within two months of the date of the child's birth, the payments may be backdated to run from the date of the birth.

The duration of a periodical payments order is until the child reaches the age of 17 (birthday after school-leaving age) but can be for longer if the court thinks it appropriate.

Either party can apply to have the periodical payments order varied later on or for a lump sum to be ordered if, for example, the means of one of them change. Also the child may apply once he is 16. The application to vary has to be made to the court where the original order was issued.

If the putative father dies, any order for periodical payments comes to an end. If the mother dies or marries, the payments to the child continue (but the putative father may apply for a variation). If the child gets adopted, the payments cease.

tax and maintenance payments
The order may be made payable either to the mother 'for the child's benefit' or to the child direct. If the order is for payments to the child direct, the money will count as his income for tax purposes and the child will be entitled to claim the single person's personal tax allowance, which means that no tax will be payable on the first £2,205 (1985/86 tax year).

Where the payment is direct to the child and does not exceed £33 a week or £143 a month, the order will be treated as a 'small maintenance payment' which means that the payments will be made gross. If the payments exceed these amounts, the payer will deduct tax at 30% before paying out. At the end of the tax year, a tax repayment claim can be made if more has been deducted for tax than the child is liable to pay (as will probably be the case).

If the order for payment is to the mother 'for the child's benefit' rather than to the child direct, the money will count as her income for tax purposes, and the small maintenance limit is only £18 a week or £78 a month.

When maintenance is paid under a court order, it ceases to be counted as the payer's income for tax purposes – in effect, bringing tax relief at the payer's highest rate of income tax.

– voluntary arrangement

Even if the father and the mother are in agreement as to maintenance, there are considerable advantages in obtaining a court order. If the father pays voluntarily without an enforceable agreement or a court order, he is not entitled to any tax relief.

From the mother's point of view, the small maintenance payment rules do not apply to out-of-court agreements so that tax at 30% will be deducted at source from any payment, irrespective of the amount, and cannot be claimed back if it is more than the tax she is liable to pay.

If the agreement is to pay to the mother for the child's benefit, the payments will become the mother's income for tax purposes, thus losing the benefit of the child's personal tax allowance.

It may therefore be worth applying for an affiliation order even though the mother is living with the father on perfectly good terms but not married to him. The father would then be able to claim tax relief on any payments ordered against him, thus enabling him to get a tax subsidy for maintaining his children (which is not available to married parents). Some tax inspectors may not be prepared to accept such an arrangement without some persuasion.

in Scotland: affiliation

It is not necessary for the mother to qualify as 'single' for the purposes of raising an action of affiliation and aliment in Scotland but she has a heavy onus to rebut the presumption that the child is not the child of her marriage.

It is possible to raise the action even before the birth of the child under the terms of the Illegitimate Children (Scotland) Act 1930; any decree for alimentary payments will not come into force until after the birth. There is no time limit for making a claim for affiliation and aliment in Scotland although delay in raising proceedings may make proof more difficult.

The action is normally raised in the sheriff court of the sheriffdom where the alleged father resides. It is usually advisable to consult a solicitor in connection with raising such an action, and legal aid can be applied for.

The mother may be assisted in proving her case by a unique provision in scottish law which relaxes the rule of corroboration in connection with such actions in recognition of the difficulty of proof. It is known as the 'doctrine of false denial' by which evidence by a defender which is disbelieved or proved false may justify an unfavourable inference, particularly where the pursuer's contrary evidence is supported. Under the terms of the Affiliation Orders Act 1952, the obligation of the father of an illegitimate child to provide aliment ceases when the child attains the age of 16 (or 18 if undergoing full-time education). An action may be raised by a pupil child's tutor *ad litem* if the mother is dead or missing.

a lone parent

If the mother is not married to the father of her child and not living with him, or married parents have separated or are divorced, the following organisations can provide advice and help:

National Council for One Parent Families (255 Kentish Town Road, London NW5 2LX, telephone: 01-267 1361)
offers free and confidential help to lone parents and single pregnant women. Publications include a question-and-answer booklet *Legal rights of single mothers* (95p but free to single pregnant women or new single mothers).

Gingerbread (35 Wellington Street, London WC2E 7BN, telephone: 01-240 0953)
is a national self-help association for one parent families with local groups throughout the country where lone parents meet other people who are also bringing up children alone, to share experiences, skills, knowledge and information about welfare and legal rights.

Families Need Fathers (BM Families, 27 Old Gloucester Street, London WC1N 3XX, telephone: 01-852 7123)
is a society for equal parental rights which, despite its name, provides counselling and advice for both parents, mothers and fathers, going through separation and divorce. It publishes booklets on problems encountered by parents apart from their children.

Child Poverty Action Group (1 Macklin Street, Drury Lane, London WC2B 5NH, telephone: 01-242 9149 and 3225)
includes among its many publications *National welfare benefits handbook* (1985 edition £3.50) and *Rights guide to non-means-tested social security benefits* (1985 edition £3.50).

In Scotland, organisations which can provide specialist advice and assistance are
Scottish Council for Single Parents, 13 Gayfield Square, Edinburgh EH1 3NX (telephone: 031-556 3899) and 39 Hope Street, Glasgow G2 6AE (telephone: 041-248 3488)
Scottish Gingerbread, 39 Hope Street, Glasgow G2 7DW (telephone: 041-248 6840).

cash help from the state

Supplementary benefit (SB) is for anyone not in full-time work (i.e. working less than 30 hours a week); family income supplement (FIS) is for parents in full-time work (i.e. working 30 hours a week or more) but a single parent is eligible for FIS if working only 24 hours a week or more. So, a single parent with a low income who is working for more than 24 hours but less than 30 hours a week has a choice whether to claim supplementary benefit or family income supplement. (DHSS leaflet NI248 discusses the options.)

Where the father is under a duty to maintain his child (if there is an affiliation order or any other court order) and he fails to do so, and the mother is receiving supplementary benefit, a contribution may be sought from him by the DHSS, who may, if necessary, take criminal proceedings against him for this.

A single parent with a child under 16 is not required to register as 'available for work' as a condition of receiving supplementary benefit and does not have to sign on at the local unemployment benefit office. Also, after receiving supplementary benefit for one year, a single parent will go on to the higher long-term SB rate.

A couple cohabiting on a permanent basis are treated by the DHSS as a married couple when assessing eligibility, and the 'advantages' for a single parent no longer apply. DHSS leaflet NI247: *Living together as husband and wife* gives details of the effect on social security benefits.

tax
There is a lone parent's additional personal tax allowance which either the mother or the father can claim if the child is living with that parent for the whole or any part of the year. The amount is such as to bring the personal tax allowance up to the same amount as the married man's allowance.

IR leaflet 29 deals with *Income tax and one-parent families.*

getting maintenance
If the mother and the father are married but they have separated and have started proceedings for divorce or judicial separation, either may claim maintenance from the other for the child straightaway, through the divorce court. The Consumer Publication *Divorce: legal procedures and financial facts* explains the situation in detail.

If the parents are separated but are not divorcing, she or he can apply for maintenance for a child through the magistrates' court or through the county court when applying for custody and access under the Guardianship of Minors Act.

adoption

When an adoption order is made, the adopter, to all intents and purposes, becomes the child's legitimate parent. Unlike other non-parental relationships, adoption is total, irrevocable and for life.

A natural parent can adopt his or her own child. The mother (or father) of an illegitimate child may adopt him so that he is no longer regarded by the law as illegitimate.

Adoptions are subject to strict supervision. Unless the proposed adopters are related to the child, the child may only be placed for adoption by an adoption agency, either a voluntary organisation or a local authority, approved by the Secretary of State for Social Services. It is a criminal offence to place a child for adoption informally (that is, other than through an approved agency) unless the proposed adopter is a relative – a grandparent, for example, or brother or sister of the child. The exception is, however, somewhat academic in that the court will be hesitant to allow a relative to adopt a child. If a relative or a step-parent applies to adopt, the court may treat the application as if it were for custodianship unless it is satisfied that the child's welfare will be better safeguarded by being adopted.

who may apply

Any applicant to adopt must be over 21 and domiciled in the UK.

Applications may be made by an individual, or by a married couple (only one of whom need be domiciled in the UK). A brother and sister or a cohabiting couple may not apply to adopt.

An individual applicant must normally be unmarried (this means that one of a cohabiting couple may apply). There are special circumstances in which a married person can apply singly – for example, someone who is permanently separated from a spouse.

Courts are reluctant to allow a step-parent to adopt unless this is clearly in the child's interests and involves no significant loss of or distortion of existing relationships, such as cutting out the other natural parent who has had had ongoing access or taken an active interest.

the adopters
At present, there are more would-be adopters than children for adoption (particularly healthy babies). But there are more older children awaiting adoption with special needs such as physical or mental handicap or children of different races and children who have been in local authority care.

Apart from the statutory requirements, adoption agencies (both the local authority and voluntary ones) make conditions for would-be adopters, such as their ages (generally under 35), health, income, racial background. Adoption agencies (and the courts) must always act 'with the best interests of the child in mind' (with emphasis on 'the child') – which is why prospective adopters of children not born to them have to go through stringent scrutiny and assessment to be approved as adopters. For natural parents wishing to adopt their own illegitimate children, this may not be quite so stringent but, even so, something of an ordeal.

Applicants should be prepared for the depth of the local authority's investigations. For example, there will be medical assessments and the local authority social worker must see the applicants and the child separately and together. He or she must report on other members of the family and their attitudes to the adoption; the background of the child, his family and natural parents and their attitudes to the adoption; the ability of the adopters to bring the child up throughout his childhood so as to integrate him effectively in the household and the family, and the community.

While adoptive parents are under no legal obligation to tell adopted children about their background or that they have been adopted, there is a presumption that parents will tell their children about adoption. It is unlikely that an adoption agency would accept anyone as an adoptive parent who would keep the knowledge from the child.

the child

A child cannot be adopted until he is at least 19 weeks old. Where the applicant is a parent, step-parent or relatives, or the child has been placed by an adoption agency, an adoption order cannot be made unless the child at all times during the preceding thirteen weeks has had his home with the applicants or one of them. If the applicant is anyone else, such as a foster parent, the child must be at least 12 months old before being adopted and have had his home with the applicants or one of them throughout the preceding 12 months.

Adoption agencies must provide the proposed adopters with written information about the child and his background.

consent

Before an adoption order can be made, the court must be satisfied that the parent (or a guardian) agrees freely, and with full understanding of what adoption involves.

Where the child is legitimate and both parents are alive, both must give their agreement. Any agreement given by a mother earlier than six weeks after the child's birth is invalid.

Agreement is not required from the father of an illegitimate child unless he has obtained an order giving him custody under the Guardianship of Minors Act 1971. But his views will normally be sought if he has been involved with the child and he will be made a respondent to the application (that is, given a voice) if he has taken responsibility for, or a real interest in, the child. Where the mother of an illegitimate child wants him to be adopted against the wishes of the natural father, the father can challenge this by applying for an order giving him custody of the child.

Agreement must be given either in writing or in person at the court hearing. The court will appoint a reporting officer (a probation officer or a social worker) whose duty it is to ensure that any person whose agreement is required fully understands the position, and to witness the written agreement. Where there is no agreement, the court appoints a guardian *ad litem* to report to the court on the desirability of the adoption order being made.

Even when agreement has been given, the parent can withdraw it at any time before the adoption order is made.

dispensing with consent
The court may dispense with the agreement of the parent or guardian if she or he

○ cannot be found

○ is incapable of giving consent (perhaps because of mental illness)

○ is unreasonably withholding agreement (that is, the court must be satisfied that no reasonable parent in the same position would refuse consent)

○ has persistently failed without reasonable cause to discharge her or his parental duties

○ has abandoned or neglected the child

○ has persistently or seriously ill-treated the child and it is unlikely that the child can go back safely to live with the parent.

Whether or not agreement should be dispensed with will be decided by the court at the time of the hearing of the adoption application. If the court proceeds to an adoption order without the agreement, the parent may appeal.

freeing for adoption

Because parental agreement can be withdrawn at any time before the hearing, it is possible for an adoption agency, before placing a child with proposed adopters, to apply to the court for an order declaring the child to be 'free for adoption'. The parents must consent to the 'freeing' – in the same way as they would need to agree to adoption, but the consent is asked for at an earlier stage of the proceedings.

The court must be satisfied that the 'relevant' parents have consented to freeing the child for adoption or that there are grounds for dispensing with this on the same grounds as dispensing with agreement to an adoption order. A reporting officer will be appointed. If only one parent, not both, consents to the child being freed for adoption (or if consent to free for adoption should be dispensed with), a guardian *ad litem* will be appointed by the court to investigate the circumstances. (The reporting officer and the guardian *ad litem* may be the same person.)

protecting prospective adopters from parent's change of mind

Once a parent has agreed to the adoption and an adoption order has been applied for, or an adoption agency has applied to free a child for adoption, the parent or the guardian may not remove the child from the proposed adopters without leave of the court while the application is pending.

Where a child has had his home with the proposed adopter for the preceding five years and they give written notice to the local authority that they intend to apply for adoption, no one can remove the child from the prospective adopters without the leave of the court before the adoption application is lodged or within three months, whichever is the earlier.

This last provision is particularly relevant where the child has been fostered out on a long-term basis by the local authority in whose care the child is: it prevents even the local authority removing the child until the application is heard, without permission of the court.

applying for an adoption order

In cases where the child was not placed for adoption through an approved adoption society or the local authority's adoption agency, the prospective adopters must give at least three months' written notice to the local authority of their intention to apply for adoption. This gives the local authority an opportunity to investigate the suitability of the applicant. The adopters (except where mother or father of the child) will have to provide medical reports on themselves and medical reports on the child.

Most applications are made in the local county court, but there is a broadly similar procedure in the magistrates' court, and the High Court has jurisdiction to make adoption orders.

Formal procedure is started by the prospective adopters 'filing' an application at the county court. This can be done as soon as the child is living with the prospective adopters, but the hearing cannot be until the child has been there for at least thirteen weeks. During that time, visits to the home may be made by a social worker from the local authority.

The court will fix the date for a hearing, and notify the natural parent(s) and the local authority. A guardian *ad litem* will be appointed to prepare a confidential report if the application is contested or if there are other special circumstances.

The applicant(s) must attend the hearing. This will be held before a judge in his room (or chambers) in the county court, or before magistrates sitting as a domestic court, with no members of the press or public present.

making the order

The court will only make an order if it is satisfied that in all the circumstances an adoption order is appropriate and that agreement has been given or dispensed with. The court is under a duty to give first consideration to the need to safeguard and promote the welfare of the child throughout his childhood. If appropriate to the child's age and understanding, the court will try to ascertain the wishes and feelings of the child regarding the decision and to give due consideration to them.

In certain circumstances, the court may make an interim order giving the proposed adopters custody of the child for up to two years. The courts may do this where it is genuinely unable to decide whether the adoption is the best course of action for the child. (At the end of the interim order, the would-be adopters can apply again.)

Or the court can refuse to make an adoption order and treat the application (if by a non-parent) as one for custodianship, or commit the child to the care of the local authority.

When the court makes an adoption order, it has the power to impose such conditions as it thinks fit but, in practice, it is unusual to impose conditions. In very exceptional cases, the court could make provision for the natural parent to have continued access to the child.

the effect of an adoption order

The effect of an adoption order is to extinguish all the natural parent's rights and duties relating to the child and vest them in the adoptive parents. The child is treated in law as if he were their legitimate child, not the child of any other parents. An adopted child takes the surname of the adoptive parents.

An adopted child cannot marry either of his or her adopters but there is nothing to prevent him or her from marrying any other relative by adoption – for example, a sister or a brother.

Under the intestacy rules, an adopted child ranks equal with a natural child for inheriting property – but cannot inherit a title.

An adoption order has the effect of bringing to an end any order for maintenance from the natural parent or an affiliation order. It also brings to an end any local authority care order or supervision.

An adoption agency may have an approved adoption allowance scheme enabling payment to be made to the adoptive parents if the child has special needs – for instance, is handicapped – or is older than the usual age for adoption.

registering the adoption

A copy of the adoption order is sent by the court to the Registrar General in London. It contains all the details about the adoption, including the child's original name and the names of his natural parents and the name by which the child will from now on be known.

The Registrar General keeps a separate adopted children register, and also a register from which it may be possible to trace an adopted child's natural parents. This information is not available to the public. But, once he or she is over 18, an adopted person has the right to have access to this information and to obtain the original birth certificate.

In the first instance, adult adoptees who want to find out about their original birth record should write to:

The General Register Office
Adopted Children Register
Segensworth Road
Titchfield
Fareham
Hants PO15 5RR

The applicant adopted before 12 November 1975, must, however, have a counselling interview before the information will be released. This counselling may be done by the General Register Office or by the local authority where he now lives or in whose area the court which granted the adoption order is, or by the adoption agency which arranged the adoption. Anyone adopted after November 1975 will, when the time comes, have the choice whether or not to be counselled.

An adopted person wanting to marry before the age of 18, who is concerned lest he or she would be marrying a close relative can write to the Registrar General and ask to be told whether the marriage would come within the prohibited degrees of kindred or affinity.

The **National Organisation for Counselling Adoptees and their Parents (NORCAP)**, (49 Russell Hill Road, Purley, Surrey CR2 2XB) is a support group for adult adopted people and for their adoptive and their natural parents. NORCAP helps adoptees wanting to trace their natural parents, but is not a tracing agency. It will not assist natural parents in active searching for adopted children, but will put their details on a contact register in case the sought person gets in touch with NORCAP. Membership is £4.50 in the first year, £3 thereafter and includes a quarterly newsletter.

sources of information

Most social services departments of local authorities act as approved adoption agencies and are required to provide some form of adoption counselling service (ask for the fostering and adoption section).

Voluntary adoption agencies such as Dr. Barnardo's, the Diocesan Catholic Children's Societies, the Church of England Children's Society, the National Adoption Society, the National Children's Home, offer a counselling and advice service for adopters, would-be adopters and parents wishing to have their child adopted.

There are various organisations concerned with adoption who can provide help and advice on all aspects. These include

British Agencies for Adoption and Fostering (BAAF) (11 Southwark Street, London SE1 1RQ, telephone: 01-407 8800; and 23 Castle Street, Edinburgh EH2 3DN, telephone: 031-225 9285) produce many relevant leaflets and publications such as the booklet *Adopting a child* (£1.50) which includes a list of adoption agencies (voluntary lay and religious and local authority) throughout the country, and the service 'Be my parent' which is a photolist of children with special needs for whom new families are being sought (updated every month).

Parents for children (222 Camden High Street, London
NW1 8QR, telephone: 01-485 7526)
is concerned with finding adopters for hard-to-place children.

Parent to parent information on adoption services (PPIAS)
(Lower Boddington, Daventry, Northants NN11 6YB, telephone:
0327 60295)
puts prospective and existing adopters in touch with one
another to provide information and practical support through
a network of over 90 co-ordinators in the UK. PPIAS annual
subscription is £4 including a newsletter 3 times a year which
has detailed information about children waiting for adoption.

In Scotland, there is a **Scottish Adoption Advice Centre** for
individual counselling and advice at 21 Castle Street,
Edinburgh EH2 3DN (telephone: 031-225 3666) and at 21 Elmbank
Street, Glasgow G2 4TV (telephone: wednesdays 2 to 5, 6.30 to 9,
041-339 0772).

education

The Education Act 1944 makes it the duty of the parent to ensure that every child receives 'efficient full-time education suitable to his age, ability and aptitude, either by regular attendance at school or otherwise' from the start of the school term after his fifth birthday until the child reaches school leaving age at 16 years. Children who reach the age of 16 between 1 February and 31 August may leave on the friday before the last monday in May. The child may not be withdrawn from school before this date even if he has a job to go to.

Parents have the right to choose whether the school a child goes to is a publicly maintained (state) school or a private (independent) school, or whether to educate their child at home.

The educational system is a national one, but locally administered. Responsibility for the education service in England and Wales is distributed between central government (the Department of Education and Science (DES) and the Education Department of the Welsh Office), the local education authorities (LEAs), the churches and other voluntary bodies, the governing bodies of educational institutions, and the teaching profession. In Scotland, responsibility lies with the Scottish Education Department under the auspices of the Scottish Office in Edinburgh, and the nine regional councils according to area.

The duty of the LEAs is the day-to-day running of the publicly maintained education service: they provide the schools and colleges in their areas and administer them. Local authorities have to arrange for sufficient places to be available in schools in order that all of the children living within their boundaries should be able to secure, through attending those schools, an education suitable to their ages, abilities, and aptitudes.

LEAs have a duty to provide full-time education up to the age of 19 (the date of the birthday) for students who request it.

Local responsibility for the curriculum rests with the individual authority (or school governing body, as the case may be): the timetabling of subjects, the choice of textbooks and the detailed content and method of day-to-day teaching are largely left to the discretion of headteachers and their staffs.

under the state education system

You cannot:

o insist that your child be admitted to school earlier than the first day of the term starting after his fifth birthday (but some LEAs will arrange earlier admission)

o insist that your child is taught at a particular school

o exercise control over what subjects your child is taught and the method by which they are taught

An exception is that subjects should not be allocated according to sex – such as woodworking for the boys only and cooking only for the girls. If this is so, you can report the discrimination to the Equal Opportunities Commission (Overseas House, Quay Street, Manchester M3 3HN or 249 West George Street, Glasgow G2 4QE).

o withdraw your child from any class (including sex education) other than religious instruction

o insist that your child sits particular CSE or O-level examinations, or takes O-level rather than CSE exams (but you can pay for private entry)

o insist that your child does not participate in games (unless there are sound medical reasons)

○ have access to confidential school records relating to your child if the school has not opted for 'open access' policy

○ control disciplinary procedures, which may include corporal punishment. (Some LEAs no longer allow corporal punishment; where allowed, it must be moderate and reasonable.)

You can:

○ insist that the local education authority provide you with details of all the schools in their area, their admission policies and planned admission targets

○ insist on details from individual schools on certain prescribed matters – for example, curricula, teaching staff, exam results, homework requirements, extra-curricular activities, policy on punishment. (Scholls now publish brochures containing this information.)

○ express a preference for the school that you wish your child to attend. The local education authority must comply with the request unless

– compliance with that preference would prejudice the provision of efficient education or the efficient use of resources

the preferred school is an aided or special agreement school and compliance with the preference would be incompatible with any arrangements between the governors and the local education authority in respect of the admission of children to that school

– admissions to the preferred school are based wholly or partly on selection according to ability or aptitude and compliance with the parents' preference would be incompatible with the selection arrangements

The LEA must arrange for parents to have the opportunity to appeal if they are not offered their preferred school.

○ withdraw your child from religious worship and religious education classes. (Religious education is the one subject which a school must teach – and each day must start with an act of worship.)

○ insist on free transport if your child is under 8 and lives more than 2 miles away from school, or is 8 or over and lives more than 3 miles away from school. (Local education authorities have a discretion to provide free or subsidised transport for children living within the 2 or 3 mile radius if they agree that this is necessary – for example, if the route is dangerous; they must provide transport for all pupils where public transport is non-existent, whatever the distance involved, but the parents may have to pay for this.)

○ require free school meals for your child if you are receiving supplementary benefit or family income supplement, or your income is low

○ have access to the school's board of governors. (Parents have a right to make a formal complaint if they believe that a head has been unreasonable. In serious cases of disagreement, they are entitled to complain further to the chief education officer of the LEA.)

○ stand for election as a governor of the school your child attends. (All LEA schools have to have a number of parents of current pupils on the board of governors; headteachers are responsible to the governors.)

A *Which?* report on *State schools: your rights* was published in February 1983.

The **Advisory Centre for Education** (18 Victoria Park Square, London E2 9PB, telephone: 01-980 4596)
gives free advice by letter or telephone to parents with children in state schools. ACE publishes a bi-monthly bulletin for anyone concerned with education (annual subscription £7.50), and a range of guides to the education service, including *Choosing a school* (£2), *Guide to education law* (£2), *School choice appeals* (£2).

Amongst the lists and publications available from the **National Children's Bureau** (8 Wakley Street, London EC1V 7QE) is a list giving details of various organisations concerned with aspects of education, both practical and campaigning, in the state and independent systems.

A parent's guide to education, published by the Consumers' Association, covers the whole range of the educational system.

private schooling

Parents who want to send their child to an independent fee-paying school are entitled to do so if they can afford it. In some schools, what the parents can afford is not necessarily the determining factor.

The assisted places scheme has been set up by the government to give help with tuition fees at certain independent secondary schools to parents who could not otherwise afford them. A leaflet *Assisted places at independent schools*, issued by the DES, describes the main features of the scheme and how a list of participating schools may be obtained.

Fee-paying schools are independent of the local education authority but have to be registered with the Department of Education and Science. When it opens, any new school is automatically given 'provisional registration' until a check can be made on its standards. Within a few terms, a decision is made by the DES as to whether it meets the minimum standards for registration to be confirmed as 'final' in terms of what it provides by way of

- premises
- accommodation
- instruction
- personnel.

A school which fails on any of these counts is liable to action which may lead to its being struck off, but so long as minimum standards in these four areas are attained, the government has no power to regulate what the schools do or how they do it.

A *parent's guide to education* says that ". . . . registration does not imply that a general inspection has been made by HM Inspectorate, and schools must simply meet the following criteria:

○ that they fulfil the requirements of the Education Acts applicable to similar LEA schools

○ that they provide a 'progressive general education' for an age-span of at least three years

○ that they have a 'suitable and efficient' teaching force at least comparable in quality and quantity to that found in LEA schools

○ that they have 'adequate' premises."

The **Independent Schools Information Service** (56 Buckingham Gate, London SW1E 6AG, telephone: 01-630 8793) gives information and advice to parents on behalf of the leading associations of independent schools. ISIS publishes a series of leaflets and a paperback guide *Choosing your independent school* (£3.50). Eight regional ISIS offices produce their own handbooks covering the UK and Eire.

not going to school

Once the child is registered at school, it is the parent's duty to ensure that he attends regularly. If he does not, the local education authority has the right to prosecute and, on conviction, the parent can be fined or eventually imprisoned. Any person in actual custody of the child may be prosecuted, not just a parent. The local education authority can bring care proceedings or the magistrates may direct the local authority to bring care proceedings in the juvenile court. If the child is considered beyond parental control, a supervision order or care order may be made.

education other than at school

Parents who do not want their child to be educated through the school system may make arrangements for the child to be educated at home. The parents have to be able to prove to the satisfaction of the local education authority that the home education provided is suitable to the child's age, ability and aptitude.

One function of the LEA's powers to enforce school attendance is to enable the child's best interests to be protected from the exercise of parental whim. If you fail to prove that your child is receiving efficient full-time education, the LEA may eventually serve a school attendance order on you and take you to court if you defy the order.

Education Otherwise (enquiries secretary at 25 Common Lane, Hemingford Abbots, Cambs PE18 9AN, telephone: 0480 63160) is a self-help organisation which can offer support, advice and information to families practising or contemplating home-based education as an alternative to schooling. There is a network of voluntary local co-ordinators who can give personal advice to members in their area, to help establish what is best suited to the needs of a particular child and family. Membership is £10 a year and includes a bi-monthly newsletter and a copy of the booklet *School is not compulsory*.

when things go wrong in the family

When things go wrong to the extent of the parents splitting up, the decision has to be made where and with whom the children will live. If the parents cannot decide between themselves, as a last resort, the court may decide.

conciliation

There are conciliation or mediation agencies now available to be invoked where difficulties arise over arrangements for children. The basic role of the conciliator is to get both parents together and help them try to work out a decision about the future of their children which is acceptable to both, without bringing pressure to bear on either.

There are basically two kinds of conciliation scheme – 'in court' and 'out of court'.

'In court' schemes are run in conjunction with divorce county courts. In most such schemes, the judge or registrar refers the dispute to the court welfare officer. (In the Divorce Registry in London, conciliation appointments are automatic in contested applications.)

'Out of court' schemes are generally run on a voluntary basis. If you think conciliation may help at any stage, you can ask your local citizens advice bureau or your solicitor to refer the case to the nearest conciliation service or you can contact one directly without being referred by anyone. The people providing this service are independent and do not act for either side or the court and offer a different approach to that of negotiation via solicitors.

The **National Family Conciliation Council** (c/o Magistrates' Court, Princes Street, Swindon SN1 2JB, or telephone 0793 27285) can give information about affiliated conciliation services and where they operate.

In Scotland
In Scotland, so far there are conciliation services in three major regions with plans to set up similar provision in other areas.

There is a full-time service based in Edinburgh operating in Lothian and another to be set up in Glasgow from November 1985 to cover the Strathclyde region. There is a part-time service based in Stirling for Central region.

These services all have trained conciliators and operate as independent voluntary organisations and have charitable status. Unlike England, none of these services is formally attached to the court but work closely with the legal profession.

Anyone wishing to use the services of any of the existing conciliation agencies in Scotland should contact the **Scottish Family Conciliation Service (Lothian)** (127 Rose Street South Lane, Edinburgh EH2 5BB, telephone: 031-226 4507).

custody, care and control, access

Legal custody means the right to make major long-term decisions for a child, mainly connected with education, medical care, moral and religious upbringing, marriage. Actual custody (also called 'care and control') indicates the right and duty to look after the child on a day-to-day basis. An access order confers the right of the parent with whom the child is not living to go on seeing the child. Strictly, access is the child's right to see the adult, and not the other way round.

Disputes over custody and access can be referred by either or both parents to the court for a decision. Whatever the situation, the court basically has to decide with whom the children shall live and who is to have custody, what rights, if any, the other parent is to have, and to decide to what extent access should be granted. The court will then issue the appropriate orders.

agreement about custody
Parents who are divorcing or separating can continue to hold parental rights jointly without any order of the court. Where the children are to live and how often they are to visit the other parent can be dealt with by informal arrangement. But on divorce, whenever children of the family are involved, a decree cannot be made absolute unless a judge has certified that he is satisfied about the arrangements for them. The courts will commonly respect the parents' agreed arrangements, but they are not bound to do so.

how the court decides

When a husband and wife are divorcing (or bringing proceedings for judicial separation or nullity), it is the divorce county court which can make orders in respect of children of the family. 'Children of the family' are children under the age of 18 and include natural children of husband and/or wife, adopted children, any other child who has been treated by both husband and wife as part of their family, including stepchildren, but not a child fostered through a local authority or voluntary organisation.

In other situations, the county court or the magistrates' court has power to make orders in respect of children. (There is no equivalent provision in Scotland.)

Whatever the proceedings, the court has to regard the welfare of a child under the age of 18 as the first and paramount consideration, and shall not take into consideration whether the claim of the father or that of the mother is superior to that of the other parent. This 'welfare principle' takes precedence over every other factor so that the court will not be interested, for example, in who was to blame for breaking up a marriage unless that person's conduct seriously reflects on his or her abilities as a parent.

The factors that the court will take into account in coming to a decision will broadly be the same, whichever the court.

○ As a matter of practice, the mother will have the care of very young children. The courts award the care of young children to the father only in very unusual circumstances – for example, if the father convinces the court that the children's mother is for some reason wholly unsuited for bringing up the children or that he is considerably more suited. If the children are older – say, over 8 years – the court may accept that, for example, boys are perhaps better brought up by their father. Courts are now more willing to accept the situation of a man giving up work to look after his children.

○ The courts generally lean towards preserving the status quo. If a child has been living with one parent for any length of time, the court will be very hesitant to change this arrangement. This is why generally young children stay with their mother.

○ It is generally thought that it is better for brothers and sisters to grow up together. So the court will be reluctant to split up children.

○ The older the child becomes, the more his preferences are likely to be an influencing factor, but the courts are reluctant

to place any child in the invidious position of choosing
between his parents. A High Court or county court judge
may interview a child (magistrates do not have this power)
on his own but rarely does so unless the child is at least 8
years old. The court may on occasions regard it as in a child's
best interests to override his own wishes, but once a child
is in his teens, it is generally accepted as impracticable and
counter-productive to force the child to live with a parent
against his wishes.

o Where the conduct of one of the parents is directly relevant
   to the welfare of the child (for example, if the father has been
   convicted of an indecent assault), this would be a crucial
   factor on the issue of custody and also of access. If the parent
   who wishes to have the care of the children is cohabiting
   with anyone, the character of the cohabitee will be
   considered. If one of the parties is a practising homosexual
   or lesbian, such a relationship may be considered a strong
   influencing factor.

o The ability to provide a comfortable and adequate home and
   provide for the child's other material needs is an important
   factor. On divorce, the matrimonial home usually goes to
   whoever has care of the children. Because the care of young
   children is generally given to the mother, the father usually
   cannot compete in terms of offering suitable accommodation.

o Continuity of care is another important factor: a parent who
   is out at work all day may have more difficulty in offering
   adequate care than one who is not. If a child is to be cared
   for jointly with some third party, perhaps a relative or
   someone with whom one of the parties has formed a new
   relationship, the court will want to have an opportunity of
   weighing up this new substitute parent to see whether he or
   she can offer adequate care.

Each case is different, however, and the facts of each will be
weighed up by the court.

joint custody?

In divorce proceedings, the court can make a joint custody order with 'care and control' being given to one parent and 'reasonable access' to the other. This provides for the child to be physically nurtured by the parent given care and control, with all the major decisions – for example, on religion or education – remaining vested in the parents jointly. The parent who has care and control is the one who controls the children's day-to-day lives – for example, when they can watch TV – and the other parent cannot interfere, despite the joint custody order.

Generally, a couple will secure an order for joint custody if they and the court think they can agree on most issues in respect of their children and if they are able and willing to co-operate over their children. But if there is dissension between them over the children, as well as in respect of their own relationship, the court is likely to order custody only to the parent who will be looking after the children on a day-to-day basis (that is the parent with care and control). The other parent will, however, have the right to return to the court in the event of a major dispute. In fact, a parent always has the right to ask the court to review any major decision by the other – such as a choice of school or religion – even if he or she does not have a custody order in his or her favour.

In non-divorce proceedings it is not possible for the court to make a joint custody order: legal custody can be granted only to one parent, with specified rights retained by the other.

decisions on access

The courts have wide powers regarding access. The court may

○ merely order 'reasonable access' and leave it to the parties to make arrangements between themselves (this happens on divorce if a couple agree, for example, that their children will make their main base with their mother, visiting their father regularly); or

○ include specific provisions – for example, that the child should spend some time away from home with the non-custodial parent ('staying or residential access') or that the non-custodial parent should merely be entitled to see the child and take him out ('visiting access'); or

○ specify where access should take place – for example, at the grandparents' house – or that the child should see a parent who has moved abroad initially only in this country; or

○ if the parents cannot agree between each other, specify the periods of access – for example 'visiting access 10 a.m. to 5 p.m. every other sunday' or 'staying access for two weeks during every summer holiday' ('defined access'); or

○ in extreme cases, arrange for access to take place initially under the supervision of a probation officer or social worker ('supervised access'); this would normally be ordered only as a last resort and as a short-term measure.

Parents can vary the access arrangements by agreement between each other or, if there is a dispute, can go back to the court and ask for a variation of the order.

– access denied
Only in exceptional circumstances will the court refuse access to a parent: for example, where a parent has sexually assaulted the child or where the child is severely emotionally disturbed by seeing the parent, and attempts to overcome this have repeatedly failed.

If the parent with whom the child lives creates difficulties over access or tries to prevent it, the other cannot do much about it except to return to the court. The intervention of a court welfare officer may be helpful, as may in-court or out-of-court conciliation. In theory, the person who refuses to comply with an access order can be imprisoned; in practical terms, the court is most unlikely to order this. But if a court is aware that a parent is deliberately trying to flout the order for the other parent to have access, it may warn that a continuation of this behaviour could result in the court ordering that the child live with the other parent.

welfare reports and other evidence

Where there is any dispute, the court will usually order a welfare officer's report. In the Divorce Registry in London, and in some divorce county courts, there is a specific court welfare unit; in other courts, the report will be prepared by a probation officer. He or she will see the children at least once alone, and if possible also in the presence of each parent. Both parents will be interviewed and so will any third parties who are important in the child's life – for example, relatives, the children's school teacher, the family doctor. The person preparing the report will investigate the home circumstances and the respective capabilities of the parties, and how the children relate to them. The welfare officer's report is a crucial factor in any custody or access dispute.

The parents (and their legal advisers) are entitled to see a copy of the report but the contents may not be disclosed to any other person. It is important to ask the court for a further report if you feel the welfare officer has overlooked an important aspect of your child's life or, for example, has not seen the children with you at your home.

Welfare reports usually contain a recommendation and, in practice, the court will follow this recommendation although it does not have to. If you disagree with any of the welfare officer's conclusions, you can ask that he or she should be at the court hearing to be cross-examined (if so, advance warning should be given as far ahead as possible).

If either party wants to bring before the court a report from an expert (for example, a child psychiatrist or paediatrician), the consent of the other party or the court must be obtained. Medical experts should normally be instructed by both parties jointly because the expert is giving independent evidence rather than being called on behalf of one party or the other. In any event, the use of experts is bound to be expensive.

In Scotland, the position is rather different in that there is no specialised court welfare service or probation office. Should the court decide that it would be desirable to obtain a report (the parties cannot insist on this being done), the sheriff or judge will make an order of court compelling one of the parties to be responsible for instructing the report from an advocate (if the action is raised in the court of session) or a solicitor (if the action is in the sheriff court), or from an area social work department if the circumstances of the case indicate that this would be more appropriate. Neither of the parties can insist that the reporter be present to challenge the accuracy of the report at any subsequent hearing. A report is usually only obtained in order to assist the sheriff or judge in making an interim decision until the case is heard in full when witnesses for each side will be called. Either party can lodge whatever expert evidence he or she thinks necessary, without the consent of the other party. If the case proceeds to a full hearing, the expert will have to be present in court to speak to any report.

applying for custody or access

A right to apply to the courts depends on your status in relation to the child and, if a parent of the child, your marital status.

Parents who are in the process of divorce apply to the divorce county court as part of the divorce proceedings. Parents who have separated but are not, as not yet, divorcing may apply to the county court or the magistrates' court.

Either the mother or father of a child under the age of 18 can apply for legal custody or access, under the Guardianship of Minors Act 1971. The parents do not have to be married to each other, so this Act enables the father of an illegitimate child to apply for custody of or access to the child. The category of children to which the 1971 Act applies is much narrower than in proceedings under the other statutes: the court has jurisdiction only to resolve disputes between parents regarding their natural or adopted children, but not 'children of the family' such as a child by a former marriage of a woman with whom a man is living but has not married.

Third parties – for example, a grandparent or a relative – have very limited rights to initiate custody proceedings. Grandparents will not be granted an order for access unless there is a court order for legal custody or where one or both of the child's parents has died.

If there is any contest about custody or access, you should seek legal advice and may need a solicitor to represent you in court.

The **Solicitors Family Law Association** (secretary at 154 Fleet Street, London EC4A 2HX) is an association of matrimonial lawyers who subscribe to a code of practice designed to encourage and assist parties to reconcile differences and wherever possible to avoid conflict. You can ask the secretary of the SFLA for a list of members in your region.

Application for an order may be made to the High Court or the county court or the magistrates' court. In practice, however, the magistrates' court is likely to be used most frequently because it is cheaper. If legal aid is being applied for, the legal aid authorities will be unlikely to grant legal aid for proceedings in the higher courts with their attendant expense unless there is some very good reason.

procedure in the magistrates' court

The applicant goes to the magistrates' court for the area in which he or she lives to 'make a complaint' under the Domestic Proceedings and Magistrates' Courts Act 1978. This is done by completing a form available from the magistrates' court, on which you can ask for custody and/or financial provision.

Financial provision will be ordered on the basis that the other party has failed to provide for or to make proper contribution towards the reasonable maintenance of a child of the family.

The parent of an illegitimate child can apply similarly under the Guardianship of Minors Act 1971 for custody or access but not for maintenance.

what orders

In deciding any question of custody or upbringing, the court must treat the welfare of the child as the first and paramount consideration.

The magistrates have power

○ to grant legal custody to one person and access to the other parent or any other person (such as a grandparent)

○ to grant custodianship to a non-parent

○ to commit a child to the care of the local authority or make a supervision order.

The court may make an interim custody order which preserves the status quo where it is not in the children's interests to be kept in limbo and where the *de facto* custodial parent needs an order for extra status (for example to get rehoused by the local authority).

The court has power to make an order prohibiting the removal of a child of the family from England and Wales whenever it makes an order for legal custody or interim custody.

Magistrates can order one party to pay a lump sum (maximum £500) and/or periodical payments to or for a child. (The tax advantages of payments 'to' the child are the same as in the case of an affiliation order.)

When deciding how much maintenance to order for a child, the court has to consider the child's financial needs, any mental or physical disability, his income and earning capacity, and that of the parents, the standard of living enjoyed by the family and the manner in which the parties had planned for him to be educated or trained. If a child of the family is not the natural child of the person being asked to pay, the magistrates also take into account the basis on which he has assumed responsibility for the child's maintenance, whether he knew that the child was not his own, and the liability of any other person to maintain the child.

The court can make an order on the terms of an agreement already reached by the parties, but is not bound to respect the parties' agreement.

the hearing

There are special provisions to ensure that (unless the child is an adopted one) any parent who is not a party to the proceedings must be notified of the proceedings and no order may be made unless he is present or the court is satisfied that he has been notified of the proceedings.

The proceedings will be heard by magistrates sitting as a domestic court. All the issues will be dealt with at one hearing (rather than separate hearings dealing with custody and with maintenance, as is often the case in divorce proceedings). There is no evidence on affidavit (that is, a sworn statement made by a person not present at the court). Anyone who wishes to give evidence must attend and give oral evidence on oath.

If any members of the press are present, what they are allowed to report is strictly limited.

procedure in the divorce court

A husband or wife when filing a petition for divorce (or judicial separation) must complete a 'statement as to arrangements for children' (a printed form is available from the court office). On this must be given details of the proposed arrangements for any children of the family under the age of 16, or under the age of 18 if still at school or college, or training for a trade, profession or vocation (even if the child is also earning). The judge will have to declare that he is satisfied with the arrangements for such children before a decree nisi can be made absolute. One or both parents have to attend before the judge to discuss the arrangements. In some cases, the judge may require a welfare officer's report – for instance, if it is proposed that the child lives with a third party or with the parent with whom he has not been before the divorce.

If there is no dispute about custody and where the child is to live, the judge makes the appropriate orders at the same time as certifying his satisfaction.

Where there is dispute, both parents will be required to swear affidavits and also to obtain affidavits from any other witnesses whose evidence they wish the court to have.

The court may make an interim order at any stage in the proceedings (and even if the divorce petition is dismissed). This may be necessary if, for example, an emergency arises where a child has been snatched by the other parent.

Contested custody and access hearings can become extremely expensive and the sheer process of fighting over the children may make it almost impossible for parents to continue to discuss matters affecting their children reasonably, and

co-operate in the interest of the children. If you cannot reach
agreement, consult a conciliator or a solicitor, if necessary, who
is a member of the Solicitors Family Law Association. Out of
court agreement is always preferable unless you have real fears
for your child should you concede or reach a compromise.

what orders
The divorce court has virtually unlimited discretion as to how
custody, care and control and access of any child of the family
should be allotted. The court will rarely exclude one or other
parent altogether.

It may make an order for joint custody with care and control to
one parent and access to the other. The court may impose
conditions about access (for example, that the child should not
have contact during an access visit with a specified third party)
but courts generally prefer to avoid imposing conditions and
try to leave the parties to sort things out for themselves.

Should a grandparent wish to have custody or access, he or she
may apply to the court for 'leave to intervene'. The court will
decide on the basis of what is best for the child.

A supervision order can be made in matrimonial proceedings,
or a child can be committed to local authority care.

– leaving the country
The custody order contains a provision that while they are
under 18 the children must not be removed from England and
Wales (which means that they cannot be taken to Scotland,
Northern Ireland, Channel Islands, Isle of Man as well as not to
foreign countries) unless

○ the court gives leave
or
○ the written consent of the other parent is obtained and the
parent who wishes to take the child abroad gives a written
undertaking to return him when called upon to do so.

Trips abroad for holidays should not cause any great problems,
but difficulties can arise where the parent with whom the

children live remarries and wishes to emigrate and take the children. In such a case, the court will, as always, be concerned first and foremost with what is in the best interests of the children. This means that the court may, in appropriate cases, authorise a child being taken to live abroad even though this may have the effect of cutting off access to the other parent.

At any stage in divorce proceedings, either parent can apply for an injunction restraining the other from removing any child from the jurisdiction.

You should get a solicitor's help with an application for an injunction. (The 'green form' legal advice scheme allows for a solicitor's advice about applying for an injunction.) Similarly, if an injunction is served on you, you should get legal advice.

The cost of obtaining an injunction is likely to be some hundreds of pounds. Legal aid is available for a solicitor to make an application for an injunction and it is possible for an emergency legal aid certificate to be granted immediately.

An emergency application for an injunction can be heard very quickly – usually in a few days or, in a real emergency, straightaway even without written affidavit evidence.

– change of name

Any custody order automatically contains a provision that no step may be taken by the parent who has been granted custody which would result in the child being known by a new surname, except with the leave of a judge or the consent in writing of the other parent. If the parents do not agree, the court can be asked to decide the issue.

If the parent with whom the child is living seeks to change the child's surname against the wishes of the other parent to that of the new partner she has married or is living with, the other parent is entitled to apply for an injunction to prevent this. The court will decide on the basis of what is in the best interests of the child, and will not be swayed by considerations such as the wish of the custodial parent to sever all association with the other parent (unless perhaps his surname has notorious connotations).

Where the custodial parent has changed the child's name – for example, at school – and the other does not find out until some time later, the court will have to decide whether it is in the child's interests to leave him with his new surname or change back again.

– financial provision

On the parents' divorce, the court may order periodical payments to be made for the child and also that one of the parents pay a lump sum or transfer or settle property for the benefit of the child. The court may make orders for financial provision for a child independently of any orders for custody or access.

The court must give first consideration to the welfare of the children of the family when deciding what financial provision to order. The interests of the children come first when deciding, for example, how much maintenance to order for a wife and how the matrimonial home is to be allocated.

The Consumer Publication *Divorce: legal procedures and financial facts* contains full details of all arrangements on divorce.

in Scotland: procedure for orders for custody, access and aliment

Magistrates' courts do not exist in Scotland: the relevant courts are the court of session and the sheriff court.

Actions for custody and/or divorce may be raised either in the court of session in Edinburgh or in one of the 45 local sheriff courts. Most actions are raised in the sheriff court; it is necessary to use counsel if the action is to be raised in the court of session. Small claims for aliment must be raised as summary cause actions for payment in the sheriff court but, where custody is also at issue, it is normal to employ a solicitor in view of the type of procedure.

In Scotland, where aliment is sought, the court has no power to award a lump sum payment although the court will have regard to the same circumstances as in England when assessing any award. Joint custody of a child can be sought but this is unusual in Scotland.

Where the child is not resident with either of the parents, the person or authority having *de facto* custody must be called as a party to the action.

Insofar as custody is concerned, the procedure is much the same whether the action is presented as an integral part of a divorce action or as a separate action.

The hearing will not be in private, although it is unusual for members of the public to attend such hearings.

Where the parties agree custody, the court still requires to be satisfied that it is in the best interests of the child and normally affidavits have to be lodged to this effect or a parole proof (oral evidence from the custodial parent and another corroborating witness) has to be given to establish this to the court's satisfaction.

Where custody is in dispute, the parties must lodge formal pleadings setting out their arguments. These are normally prepared by solicitors. The court will set a date for a proof when witnesses can be brought.

Any order made will only be valid until the child reaches the age of sixteen years. Any order in relation to custody, access or aliment may be varied at any time before the child is sixteen. It is necessary to demonstrate a change of circumstances since the original application.

Breach of an order relating to custody is tantamount to contempt of court and the court may impose any penalty it sees fit.

Enforcement of orders for aliment in Scotland is undertaken by sheriff officers, who act as independent officers of the court. Normally, they prefer instructions to come from solicitors in view of the complexity of this area of law. Legal aid is available in Scotland for enforcement purposes.

step-parents

A stepfamily may come about as a result of the joining of two partners, one or both of whom has brought children from a previous relationship to the present family. Many stepfamilies are created as the result of divorce or separation, but many are also formed after the death of a partner. Stepfamilies can take a variety of forms, including those who are stepfamilies only at weekends or during holidays.

There is no formal legal status of step-parent in english law. The step-parent does not have the automatic rights of a parent unless they are granted to him or her by a court, nor does the stepchild have automatic rights of inheritance. Step-parents do have responsibilities towards stepchildren who have been accorded the status of 'child of the family' and may be required to provide financial support for stepchildren if the marriage ends.

Stepfamilies involved in custody and access disputes over children of former partners may face legal problems over the rights and obligations of step-parents.

The National Stepfamily Association (Maris House, Maris Lane, Trumpington, Cambridge CB2 2LB, telephone: 0223 841306) offers practical help, support, information and advice to all members of stepfamilies (married or unmarried, full-time or part-time, parents and children) and to liaise with all those working with stepfamilies in a professional, voluntary or academic capacity. The Association puts members in touch with one another where desired, provides access to leaflets and booklets on the problems of stepfamilies: *The Step-parent's Handbook* (£2.95) contains sections on practical legal and financial issues affecting stepfamilies. The Association runs a telephone support service in selected places for those who want to talk in confidence about their problems.

custodianship

The legal concept of custodianship was introduced by Part II of the Children Act 1975 and is effective from 1 December 1985. It can be described as a halfway house between fostering which bestows no particular legal rights on the foster parents, and adoption which provides the adoptive parents with full parental rights.

Custody and custodianship are not the same thing. Custodianship is a court order vesting 'legal custody' in a third party. A parent being given 'custody' of a child as part of divorce proceedings already has wider parental powers than a custodianship order can bestow.

Custodianship does not sever the natural tie between the parent and the child: it transfers only those parental rights and duties which relate to the person of the child; thus, a custodian has no right over a child's property.

Custodianship does not give the child a permanent place in the custodian's family. The formal relationship with the custodian ceases when the child becomes 18 or the custodianship order is revoked.

who may apply for custodianship

The primary qualification is that the child has had his home with the applicant for a specified period.

In certain cases, the applicant is only entitled to apply if the parent or guardian consents. If there is more than one parent or guardian, the consent of only one will be sufficient.

○ Anyone may apply with whom the child has been living for a period of three years, or separate periods which together add up to three years, including the three months immediately preceding the application. In this situation, no consent is required and no one (including a local authority in whose care the child is) can remove the child from the applicant without consent or the leave of the court.

○ Anyone may apply with whom the child has had his home for a period or periods prior to the application of at least twelve months, including the three months immediately preceding the application, provided the applicant has the consent of at least one parent or guardian.

○ A relative or step-parent with whom the child has had his home for the three months preceding the application may apply, provided a parent or a guardian consents.

Quite apart from these three categories, the court has power to appoint a third party as custodian in proceedings brought by a party to a marriage or a parent under the Domestic Proceedings and Magistrates' Courts Act 1978 or under the Guardianship of Minors Act 1971. Under the Children Act, the court may, on an application for an adoption order, make a custodianship order instead. The court can do this even where the person being appointed custodian does not meet any of the criteria for the child's preceding residence with him or her.

Relatives or foster parents may apply for custodianship and there is nothing to stop cohabitees or a brother and sister applying.

A step-parent may apply where the parent other than the one the step-parent has married is dead or cannot be found. But not allowed to apply is the step-parent of a child for whom there is a custody order arising from the divorce of the parent (now married to the step-parent) – because he or she can apply through the divorce court for the order to be varied so as to give him or her custody.

The only other people who cannot apply for custodianship are the mother or father (who may apply for custody under the Guardianship of Minors Act).

procedure

An application may be made in the High Court, or to the county court or magistrates' court.

Notice has to be given to the local authority by the applicant within seven days of making the application. The local authority has to arrange for an officer to make a report to the court about the circumstances so that the court will have the necessary information to reach a decision. The officer will need to interview the applicant, the natural parents where possible, and the child. Medical certificates are required for the applicant (unless a step-parent) and for the child.

The court must treat the welfare of the child as the first and paramount consideration. Thus, it will not necessarily put the claims of a natural parent first if this is considered not to be in the child's best interests.

Because custodianship does not automatically sever the connection between the natural parent and the child but puts the parental rights into suspension, the court has power to make orders for access to the child's mother, father or grandparent, or anyone who has treated the child as one of his or her family.

Also, the court may order, if the custodian asks for it, that the natural parent(s), or someone who has assumed responsibility for the child's maintenance, make periodical payments and/or a lump sum (limit of £500 in a magistrates' court) to the custodian.

An allowance may be paid to the custodian (except where this is a stepmother or stepfather) by the local authority, entirely at its own discretion. The allowance is likely to be made available if the child has formerly been in long-term care , or the custodianship arrangement is clearly a means of preventing the child having to be taken into care. In any case, custodians are entitled to child benefit.

Custodianship ceases when the child reaches the age of 18. Before that age, a custodianship order is revocable on the application of the custodian or of the child's mother or father or of the local authority. For this, there has to be a further court hearing.

If a custodianship order is revoked, legal custody goes back to the body or person who had it before the order was made, unless the court orders differently. If there is nobody to take on custody of the child, the court may put the child into the care of the local authority.

ward of court

Any person who has a close relationship or who can show a sufficient cause for concern can apply to have a child made a ward of court. Wardship has the effect of vesting all parental rights in the High Court. Any child under the age of 18 who is in England or Wales can be made a ward of court regardless of domicile.

The purposes for which wardship proceedings may be taken are many: for example, parents who wish to prevent their daughter having an undesirable association, grandparents who feel that their daughter is incapable of looking after their grandchild, an individual social worker or a local authority concerned about a specific aspect of the welfare of a child where its own statutory powers are insufficient. Wardship proceedings are the method of securing the return of a child who has been 'snatched' by the other parent or preventing the child's removal from England and Wales.

Wardship is commonly threatened by anxious parents but it is a practical proposition (particularly for someone who is approaching 18) only where really serious danger is envisaged.

The person applying to have the child made a ward of court must state his or her relationship to the child, and if considered inappropriate, the application will be dismissed by the court. (This rule was introduced after a case when a nightclub owner applied to have an heiress made a ward of court in order to obtain publicity for his nightclub. The summons was struck out as an 'abuse of process',)

procedure
Wardship proceedings may only be brought in the High Court. Although relatively easy to begin, wardship proceedings can be extremely expensive and should therefore not be taken without legal advice.

If you have serious cause for concern and believe wardship proceedings are necessary, consult a solicitor at once, explaining that you need immediate advice.

The great advantage of wardship proceedings is the speed and immediacy, which can give a breathing space to sort things out. In an emergency, a judge can be contacted directly, either by telephone or in person by the solicitor.

An originating summons is issued in the High Court. The effect of the issue of the summons is that the child becomes a ward immediately for 21 days. From that moment, no major decisions – for example, to move the child – can be made without the court's agreement.

Unless an appointment for a hearing of the summons is obtained within these 21 days, the child then ceases to be a ward of court.

The defendant – other parent or any other person who is involved with the child (including, if the child is old enough, the child himself) – should be sent a copy of the summons by the person who has started the proceedings. The child himself is not normally a party to the proceedings but if it is thought that he should be separately represented, the official solicitor is usually invited to represent him.

If the whereabouts of the ward are not known, a defendant is obliged to give what details he knows of the ward's whereabouts. A solicitor acting for the defendant is not covered by privilege and must therefore reveal any information that has been communicated to him by his client.

– child taken away
When a child has been taken away, an application can be made to a judge as soon as the wardship summons has been issued

for an injunction securing the child's return. (Although wardship proceedings are normally in private, the judge may in these circumstances, if the applicant wishes, arrange for the press to be present so that maximum publicity may be given.)

Where it is thought that a child who has been snatched is about to be taken out of the country, it may be possible to obtain from the court a 'Home Office letter', once a wardship summons has been issued. You can then contact the Home Office (C2 Division, Queen Anne's Gate, London SW1H 9AT, telephone: 01-213 3102 or 213 5185) and ask that a watch be kept at ports and airports. You need to be able to give the child's full names, nationality and date of birth, and those of the removing adult. It also helps to provide any information about a likely departure point and time. The Home Office should be given a 24-hour contact point.

A practical alternative procedure is to contact the local police and ask them to notify relevant ports or airports. It is easier to substantiate your case with a wardship order, but strictly the order is not necessary because it is an offence under the Child Abduction Act 1984 to attempt to remove a child from the UK without lawful authority.

in Scotland
Wardship procedure has no equivalent in Scotland. It is possible, however, for a third party to intercede on the child's behalf and ask the court to intervene against the wishes of a parent by granting an interdict to prevent the parent taking a particular course of action.

the effect of wardship

Once a child is made a ward, the High Court to all intents and purposes becomes the child's parent and may delegate any parental rights as it thinks fit. It may, for example, give the care and control to one party, stipulate arrangements as to access, give or withhold consent to the child undergoing a surgical operation or other medical treatment.

The court has power to order that either parent of a legitimate child should make periodical payments to the other parent or to whoever has care and control of the ward or to the ward himself.

A judge can commit a child who is a ward to the care of the local authority but the court still retains its supervising interest and powers.

The court's permission is required if a ward wishes to marry before the age of 18, or to leave England or Wales (even for a short visit or to go to Scotland).

If a ward of court fails to obtain the court's consent before getting married, the marriage would not be invalid but the couple would be guilty of contempt of court; the ultimate penalty for contempt of court is imprisonment.

Any attempt to remove the ward from England or Wales without the court's permission will be contempt of court (punishable by imprisonment).

Anyone wishing to change a ward's surname will need to apply to a judge who will decide this issue, as all others, on the basis of what is in the child's best interests.

The court may also exercise control over education, where and with whom the ward is to live, whom he is to visit or associate with, financial matters and, in fact, the ward's whole life: the degree to which the control is exercised in practice depends on the circumstances of the particular case.

The court may terminate the wardship at any time, and the court's jurisdiction over a ward automatically ceases at the age of 18. Even if married before the age of 18, a ward may remain subject to the court until the age of 18, although normally the court ends the wardship on marriage or adoption.

local authority care

A child under the age of 17 may come into the care of a local authority due to one of a number of circumstances:

○ a local authority may itself apply to the court for a care order

○ one or both parents may place a child voluntarily in the care of the local authority (and the local authority may pass a parental rights resolution')

○ the court in matrimonial proceedings may make a care order

○ a child who is a ward of court may be placed into the care of the local authority

○ a child who has committed an offence may be made subject to a care order.

Children in care are the responsibility of the local authority's social services department, and day-to-day matters are dealt with by the social worker in charge of the case.

care proceedings

An application for a care order may be brought by

○ a local authority social services department

○ a local education authority

○ a police officer

○ an officer of an authorised society, such as the NSPCC.

A parent cannot bring care proceedings in respect of his own child but can ask the local authority to take proceedings if the child is 'beyond parental control' (this is not defined in law).

Care proceedings are brought in the local juvenile court. This is a special magistrates' court which sits in private, with a bench of three magistrates from the juvenile panel.

An order may only be made if the applicant can prove that

○ the child is being ill-treated; *or*

○ the child's proper development is being avoidably prevented or his health is being avoidably impaired or neglected; *or*

○ it is probable that the above condition will occur because a court has found that another child of the same household has been neglected or ill-treated; *or*

○ because a person in the same household as the child has been convicted of a serious offence against a child or children; *or*

○ the child is exposed to moral danger; *or*

○ the child is beyond the control of his parent or guardian; *or*

○ the child is not receiving suitable efficient full-time education.

In addition, the applicant must establish that the child is in need of care or control and is unlikely to receive this unless the court makes an order.

Care proceedings are most frequently brought by the local authority involved, who believes that the child is being abused or neglected, or that the parents cannot cope, or that the child is clearly beyond control, or is being kept from or is persistently truanting from school.

The local authority has a duty to investigate allegations of neglect and mistreatment, and keeps a register of children thought to be 'at risk' so that the relevant people can be aware of potential problems. The register is available to a restricted group of people – for example, the police, a doctor, NSPCC inspector.

The local authority may have had a lengthy history of involvement with the family before it takes care proceedings. The decision to bring care proceedings is usually preceded by a case conference at which a number of people, including representatives from the local education authority and the police, and sometimes a local doctor, take part.

The social services department will try to reduce the need to admit a child to care (and has a duty to do so) and in exceptional circumstances can give assistance in cash or kind in order to keep children within their families.

in an emergency
Where an emergency situation flares up, a social worker can apply to a magistrate for a 'place of safety' order, authorising the applicant to remove the child and put him in a place of safety – for example, a community home or hospital. This order lasts for a maximum of 28 days, after which time the order automatically comes to an end unless the local authority or the NSPCC brings care proceedings.

A police officer has the right to remove a child to a 'place of safety' for up to 8 days without a magistrate's order. This does not cover the right to enter and search premises, unless there is a warrant.

legal representation
If the parents are financially eligible, they can get legal advice under the 'green form' scheme and can apply for legal aid for a solicitor to represent them and the child at the hearing.

Where the interests of the parents and the interests of the child are likely to be in conflict, the court may make an order prior to the hearing that the child and the parents be separately represented. In such a case, the magistrates usually appoint a guardian *ad litem* to investigate all the circumstances, interview the relevant people, and prepare a report. The guardian *ad litem* is an independent social worker with experience of child care cases who has not been involved in this case. He or she will generally instruct the solicitor appointed to act for the child under a legal aid order. Provided there is a separate representation order, the parents can also apply for legal aid (if financially eligible) in order to be represented.

The Law Society has set up a national panel of solicitors to act both for children and for parents in need of representation in child care cases. This contains the names of solicitors with experience of dealing with child care cases; many of them have attended special training courses. The clerks in all juvenile courts, panels of guardians *ad litem,* and various advice and welfare organisations, receive copies of the list. Further information can be obtained from the child care panel administrator, The Law Society, 113 Chancery Lane, London WC2A 1PL (telephone: 01-242 1222).

If the child is separately represented, the parents can, at the hearing, put questions themselves to the local authority (or police or NSPCC) in cross-examination or call evidence to rebut allegations.

If there is no order for separate representation, the parents themselves can request the court to be heard on behalf of the child.

the hearing
A child over five years old must attend the hearings as respondent unless he cannot – for example, because of illness. The parents also may be compelled to attend.

The hearing is in two stages. In the first stage or 'proof' stage, the local authority must satisfy the court that the grounds for making a care order are made out. The court will hear evidence from both parties and the parents. At the first hearing, the magistrates may make an interim order (a care order lasting for up to 28 days) and then adjourn the proceedings. If there is no interim order, the child returns home pending the next hearing.

If, and only if, the local authority proves the alleged ground, the proceedings then go into the second or 'disposal' stage, in which the magistrates read any reports and decide what, if any, orders to make.

The magistrates are likely to make

○ a care order, or

○ a supervision order (maximum length three years).

Under a supervision order, the court may lay down certain requirements, such as participation in an 'intermediate treatment' scheme. The upbringing and welfare of the child will be monitored by a social worker who will visit the home and see the child regularly. The supervisor may re-apply to the court if the supervision is not working out; in these circumstances, the court may vary the requirements of the order, or discharge it and make a care order instead.

If the parents want to appeal against a care order, the appeal has to be made in the crown court. This should not be attempted without legal advice (legal aid is available if the parents' means make them eligible). But if the child's interests were represented by a guardian *ad litem*, the child's parents have no right to appeal on the child's behalf if the guardian *ad litem* decides not to appeal.

'voluntary' care

Under the Child Care Act 1980, the local authority has a duty to receive a child under the age of 17 into care if it appears to the local authority that

○ the child has no parents or guardian; *or*

○ the child is lost or has been abandoned by parents or guardian; *or*

○ the child's parents or guardian are, temporarily or permanently, prevented from providing for his proper accommodation, maintenance or upbringing, by reason of any circumstances including mental or bodily disease or infirmity or other incapacity

provided that the local authority also considers that intervention is necessary in the interests of the welfare of the child.

In certain circumstances, if the local authority is prepared to receive the child into care, this can give a parent who is under great stress and increasingly unable to cope, a chance to recover and deal with some of the problems.

Children may be brought into voluntary care temporarily because one or other of their parents is in hospital and there is nobody to look after the child.

Local authorities are under a duty, where practicable to try to have the child's care taken over by the other parent, a guardian, or a suitable relative or friend, provided this is consistent with the child's welfare. If this is not possible, they may place the child with foster parents or in a children's home.

The voluntary nature of the arrangement is underlined by the facts that there is no court order and the child cannot be taken into care against a parent's wishes. The parent or guardian can take back the child at any time provided that the child has been in care for less than six months. Once the child has been in care for six months or more, however, the parent or guardian cannot remove the child without first giving 28 days' written notice to the local authority. The parents' right to request the child's return is, however, tempered by the local authority's ability to pass a 'parental rights' resolution at any time, and also the authority's ability to make the child a ward of court.

assuming parental rights

A local authority may pass a resolution under section 3 of the Child Care Act 1980 to assume one or both parents' parental rights over a child who has been received into care if

○ the child's parents are dead and he has no guardian or custodian; *or*

○ the parent has abandoned him (this means that the parent's whereabouts have been unknown for 12 months from the time the child was taken into care); *or*

○ the parent suffers from some permanent disability or a mental disorder which renders him or her unfit or incapable of caring for the child; *or*

○ the parent's habits or mode of life make him or her unfit to have the care of the child; *or*

○ the parent has without reasonable cause consistently failed to discharge the obligations of a parent; *or*

○ a parental rights resolution is already in force in relation to one parent and the other wants to bring the child out of local authority care but now lives, or is likely to return to live, with the parent from whom the parental rights have been taken.

Also, a parental rights resolution can be passed (provided it is in the child's interests), regardless of any other circumstances, when throughout the preceding three years the child has been in the voluntary care of the local authority or partly in care of the local authority and partly in the care of a voluntary organisation.

The social services department should, where practicable, let the parent know the reasons for the local authority's intention. A social worker should discuss the matter fully, and explain what a parental rights resolution will mean for the child's future. The parent should have the opportunity to make known any objections he or she has.

when the resolution is passed
The decision to pass a parental rights resolution is taken by the councillors on the local authority's social services committee, based on the reports and recommendations of the director of social services.

Within 72 hours of passing a resolution, the local authority must give written notice to the relevant parent, who has one month in which to object, in writing. (If you receive such a notice, you should take professional advice at once, and if at all uncertain, err on the side of caution by registering an objection within the time limit.)

If the parent does object, the resolution will lapse within 14 days unless the local authority starts proceedings in the juvenile court, in which case the magistrates decide whether or not the ground on which the resolution was passed has been made out (the burden being on the local authority to prove its case). The parent may appeal from a magistrates' order upholding a parental rights resolution to the family division of the High Court.

If a resolution is passed in respect of only one parent of a legitimate child, the local authority has to exercise parental rights or duties jointly with the other parent. (In practice, however, the local authority may assume full control over the child.)

in Scotland: local authority care

The statutory provisions enabling children under the age of seventeen to be taken into the care of the local authority in certain circumstances are to be found in the Social Work (Scotland) Act 1968. There is an obligation on the local authority to try to trace a person who might be willing to be responsible for the child's care.

Where a child is taken into care, the local authority will normally carry out a procedure whereby transfer of parental rights is accomplished. Specific grounds for the assumption of parental rights must be stated and can only be rescinded at the discretion of the local authority or by decision of the sheriff to whom application may be made for determination of the resolution of parental rights.

when a child is in care

Placing a child in voluntary care merely gives the local authority the powers needed for day-to-day care of the child, rather than transferring major parental rights, so decisions should be taken with the involvement of the parents.

A care order or a parental rights resolution vests most parental rights in the local authority but not, for example, the right to consent to adoption or to change the religion in which the child is brought up. The law is not specific about whose consent is required for the marriage of a minor who is in care.

In reaching any decision relating to a child in their care, a local authority must give first consideration to the need to safeguard and promote the welfare of the child throughout his childhood. With this proviso, the local authority has virtually unlimited discretion in deciding how best the child should be brought up (although this is limited for children in voluntary care by the parent's right to demand the child's return).

The child may be placed in a community home established by the local authority or a children's home run by a voluntary organisation, or boarded out with foster parents on a long-term or short-term basis or, quite commonly, returned to live with his parents. The local authority may regulate the extent of access to the child by a parent or guardian.

While the child is in care, the local authority should as far as is practicable find out and, having regard to the child's age and understanding, give due consideration to the wishes and feelings of the child.

The care order or resolution can remain in force until the child reaches the age of 18. If the child was already 16 when a care order was made, it can remain in force until the 'child' becomes 19. The local authority has powers and duties to help with the rehabilitation of children leaving care.

The case of every child in its care has to be reviewed by the local authority's social services department at least twice a year, to consider whether to apply for a discharge order. The local authority can rescind its own 'parental rights' resolution. The order or resolution will cease to have effect if the child is adopted or freed for adoption or marries.

the parents
Parents must maintain contact with the local authority to the extent of informing the authority of any change of address.

A parent has no basic right to control the way in which the local authority exercises its powers under a care order or parental rights resolution.

The parent does, however, have two limited rights. First, he may apply (not more than once every three months) to have the care order discharged or for a parental rights resolution to be ended, but must show the magistrates' court that there is good reason for doing this and that the child will receive the necessary care or control.

Secondly, if the local authority has either terminated access to the child or refuses to make arrangements for access, the parents has a right to apply to the court for an access order. But a parent may apply only if access is non-existent, not if he is dissatisfied with the arrangements that have been made. In most authorities there should be an established complaints procedure which parents may pursue.

There is a code of practice: *Access to children in care* (price £1.90 from HMSO) which social services departments have to follow. It says, amongst other things, that local authorities have a positive responsibility to promote and sustain access.

help and information
The **Family Rights Group** (6 Manor Gardens, Holloway Road, London N7 6LA, telephone: 01-272 4231 or 7308)
is a group of social workers, lawyers and other people who work to improve the law and practice relating to children in care. The group is concerned with the reasons why and the

manner in which children are taken into care, and the way families are treated once children have been separated from them. Annual membership is 50p for parents with children in care (£6 for others). FRG has a social worker who works with families to try to resolve their difficulties with local authorities in matters such as access, placements and involvement in decision-making, and also a solicitor who advises and represents families in legal proceedings. Publications available from FRG include a newsletter giving information about local support groups for families with children in care, which have been formed in a number of areas of the country. The Harlow group has published an informative *Guide for parents with children in care – 101 questions and answers* (75p) and *Can I see my child? – a guide to the code of practice on access* (£1), both available from Parents Aid, 66 Chippingfield, Harlow, Essex CM17 0DJ.

The National Association of Young People in Care (NAYPIC)
(second floor, The Wool Exchange, Bradford BD1 1LD, telephone: 0274 728484)
is an organisation run by and for young people in care or who have been in care, with the aim of improving conditions for young people in care and helping to start local support groups. NAYPIC provides a free information and advice service by letter and telephone. Membership is free for under 14-year-olds.

A voice for the child in care (60 Carysfort Road, Hornsey, London N8 8RB, telephone: 01-348 2588)
is a network of people concerned with children growing up in care, providing support and help with problems that arise.

Justice for Children (35 Wellington Street, London WC2E 7BN, telephone: 01-836 5917)
can offer advice on issues relating to the child care system and procedures, and juvenile justice.

financial contribution
While the child is under the age of 16, his mother and/or (if he is legitimate) his father may be required to make a weekly contribution to the child's maintenance, based on the appropriate boarding-out allowance.

Where the child is illegitimate, the local authority may apply for an affiliation order against the father; if there is an affiliation order in existence, the local authority may apply to the court that the payments made under the order be paid to the local authority.

If the child is over 16 and earning, the child himself may be required to make contributions.

with foster parents

When a child in care is boarded out with foster parents, the local authority's social services department takes responsibility for the supervision of the child in that family. Anyone is eligible to volunteer to foster, including single people. Approval of foster parents is based on a fairly rigorous assessment process, which differs from local authority to local authority. Foster parents receive a boarding-out allowance which, when a reimbursement of their costs incurred, is not subject to tax.

Minimum fostering allowances are recommended by the National Foster Care Association based on the average cost of caring for a child. Individual foster parents can join the NFCA (annual subscription £13) and get advice and information on aspects of fostering. The NFCA publications include a booklet about foster care allowances and income tax, and leaflets on general principles of fostering and on the role of the child's parent in foster care.

Publications list is available from the **National Foster Care Association,** Francis House, Francis Street, London SW1P 1DE (telephone: 01-828 6266).

Foster parents virtually have no parental rights and will have to return the child when required by the local authority even if they would like to keep the child. But, depending on the length of time the child has had his home for a continuous period with the foster parents, they may apply for adoption or custodianship.

when	*can apply for*	*condition*
after 12 months	adoption	with agreement of parent
after 12 months	custodianship	with consent of local authority
after 3 years	custodianship	no one's consent needed

private fostering

A fostering relationship can be an informal one. For example, if a child's parents die, the child's grandparents may 'foster' him without applying to the court for an order for, say, guardianship.

However, someone who is not a relative or guardian or custodian who is proposing to foster a child under the age of 16 on a long-term basis must give written notice to the local authority at least two weeks before he receives the child.

Where private fostering is an arrangement between parent and foster parent directly, the parent has to notify the local authority where the child will be living. The foster parent will be visited periodically by an officer from the local authority social services department, who has to be satisfied of the child's wellbeing. The local authority has the power to impose requirements on foster parents regarding children and may remove a child if conditions are unsuitable and may take the child into care.

Foster parents who wish to obtain parental rights, must apply to the court for adoption or custodianship or guardianship.

children and contracts

The law of contract recognises only one age barrier as being significant: the day on which a child reaches majority – the eighteenth birthday. Once your child is 18, as far as the law of contract is concerned, he is on his own, in no different position from any other adult.

While a child is under 18 (a minor), his liability in contract is extremely limited.

contracts with minors

There are two kinds of contract which are enforceable both by a minor and against him. These are

○ **contracts for 'necessaries'**
Necessaries are defined as "goods suitable to the condition in life of the minor . . . and to his actual requirements at the time of the sale and delivery." There is little authority as to what is or is not 'necessary' for, say, the average 16-year-old today – presumably because it does not cause many problems in practice. 'Necessaries' can embrace contracts for services, not only goods.

A contract cannot be enforced against a minor if it contains terms which are 'harsh and onerous'; the minor needs to pay only a 'reasonable' price if the contract price is unreasonable.

○ **contracts of employment**
  These are binding on minors if the contract is, on the whole, for the child's benefit – which is a question of fact in each particular case. (There are also statutory requirements governing the employment of children.)

Some contracts concerning property are binding on the minor unless and until repudiated by him (either before, or within a reasonable time of reaching majority) – for example, a contract for the acquisition of an interest in land or for taking a lease. Although anyone under the age of 18 cannot hold a legal estate such as the freehold of a house, a young person can rent a room or a flat on a licence agreement.

The basic position is that a minor can always sue on a contract into which he or she has entered. For example, if he bought goods and they turned out to be defective, even if they were not 'necessaries', he could sue for breach of contract just as any adult. On the other hand, the other party to a contract for the sale of goods that are not 'necessaries' cannot sue a minor for non-payment.

If non-necessaries have, in fact, been delivered to the minor, he may keep them without paying for them. He would only have to return such goods (or any identifiable proceeds if he had already disposed of them) if the minor had obtained them fraudulently – for instance, by misreprenting his age.

Money already paid by the minor, even for non-necessaries, will not be recoverable unless there has been 'a total failure of consideration', that is, the minor has received nothing of what was contracted for. This is so even if the minor has himself repudiated the contract by refusing to take delivery. So, a minor who pays a deposit but who undergoes a change of mind before delivery of goods (whether they are necessaries or not), is entitled to the return of his deposit. The effect of this is that a trader who has supplied goods to a minor on a cash-and-carry basis is not at risk of having the contract impugned on the grounds of his customer's minority.

This effectively means that anyone under the age of 18 is unlikely to be able to obtain credit because of the financial risk that this would entail for the lender, who cannot enforce payment. The lender's safeguard is to require a parent or some other adult to act as 'guarantor' indemnifying the lender or trader – as is generally the case with a hire purchase or credit sale agreement.

When a child enters into a contract, a parent cannot be liable under it unless the child was acting as the parent's authorised agent or the parent is standing guarantor for the sum involved.

Anyone under the age of 18 does not have the legal capacity to give a receipt for money paid out to him. So there would be a risk that a minor who receives money – say, under a will – can demand payment again after his 18th birthday.

The parents have the right and power to administer a child's property while he is under age, and to receive in their own name, for the benefit of the child, property or money to which the child is entitled. The parents are in the position of trustees and, strictly speaking, cannot spend the money on themselves but should only apply it for the child's benefit.

Marriage under the age of 18 does not affect a minor's contractual position, except to enlarge the category of 'necessaries' to correspond with the minor's changed status. For example, it would bring more household goods within the ambit of the definition of necessaries where a household had been set up consequent on the marriage. In particular cases, a minor could be held to have been acting as agent for an adult spouse.

In Scotland, the contractual capacity of a minor will vary according to the degree of independence the child has achieved: for instance, a minor may enter into enforceable contracts if pursuing a trade or business. The law in this field is largely governed by common law with little statutory regulation.

insurance

Minors can, and frequently do, enter into contracts of insurance – life insurance, personal accident, motor cycle and car. The opinion of insurers – and therefore their practice – differs on whether insurance is one of the necessaries for which a minor can make a binding contract. Some insurers ask for a parent's or guardian's signature on the insurance proposal form.

Motor insurance for a 16-year old's moped or a 17-year old's banger, at least to the extent to which it is compulsory under the Road Traffic Act, would probably rate as a necessary, and the minor will have to honour his side of the contract.

For a 16-year-old who sets up home, household insurance could count as a necessary. The main reservation from the insurers' point of view would be that a child may not understand the meaning of 'duty of disclosure' in the context of insurance. Household insurance proposal forms do not ask the age of the proposer. It is not clear whether the general duty of disclosure would require a young person wanting to take out household insurance to say "I am only 16 years old", even though this might influence the judgement of the underwriter.

age limits
On the proposal form for motor insurance, the age of the driver is always asked, and insurers load their premiums against a 'young' driver – but this may mean any age up to 25. Even the excess (that is the amount of damage to be borne personally) on their mother's or father's motor insurance policy is doubled or trebled if a young person was driving at the time of an accident.

There are different age limits set by different insurers for various categories of insurance, such as personal accident, private medical expenses, travel.

With holiday insurance, some insurers give cover free for children under the age of two, most limit the sum that will be paid out on the death or injury of a child, and the threshold for ceasing to count as a 'child' may be 12 or 14 or 16. Usually there will be little payment for weekly benefits under personal accident cover, because there would be no loss of earnings.

Private medical expenses schemes generally allow children to be included on the parents' family premium up to the age of 18 (or even perhaps 21).

The personal liability section of a parent's household contents policy covers a child while he is a member of the family permanently living with him. So, where the negligence of the child causes injury to someone who makes a claim against him, the claim would be met by the parents' policy.

life insurance
A life insurance policy may be taken out by a child at any age, if acceptable to the insurers and the child is old enough to know what he is doing and is acting voluntarily. But with most policies, if the child dies before a specified age (say, 12 years), the sum insured will not be paid out and only the premiums will be returned. The practice and policies of life insurance companies vary considerably. One may offer full death cover at any age if the policy is effected by trustees; another may restrict the maximum sum insured between specific ages and require the parent's signature or make it a condition that the policy cannot be surrendered before the child is 18. At the age of 18, an ex-minor may repudiate an existing life-policy and stop premium payments, but normally the premiums paid would not be returned and only a (low) cash surrender value would be paid out.

on the road

Anyone can own a car or other vehicle at any age but cannot have his name on the registration document as the 'registered keeper' until he reaches the appropriate age to drive it.

It is illegal for anyone driving any vehicle on any public road not to hold a licence.

A provisional licence to ride a moped, or equivalent machine that cannot go faster than 30 mph and with an engine capacity of no more than 50 cc, can be held from the age of 16. You must display 'L' plates until you have passed the test for a full licence.

A learner licence for a motor cycle or motor scooter with an engine capacity of no more than 125 cc can be taken out at the age of 17 but will expire after two years unless a full licence (for group D vehicles) has by then been achieved by passing a two-part motor cycle test. If you do not pass the test within two years, you will not be entitled to ride a motor cycle or scooter again until a year later. A pillion passenger must not be carried by a learner on a motor cycle unless the passenger holds a motor cycle driving licence.

At 17, a provisional licence can be taken out for driving a car. A provisional licence can be applied for (on form D.1 from the post office) before the 17th birthday; it generally takes about 3 weeks to come and is valid only from that date. A learner driver must have someone sitting beside him in the car who holds a full driving licence, and must display 'L' plates at the front and back of the car (which should be taken off when the learner is not driving).

After passing the official driving test, a provisional licence must be exchanged for a full driving licence.This will be valid up to the age of 70 without needing to be renewed.

At the age of 17 there are restrictions on what size vehicle may be driven – for example, not a goods vehicle over 3.5 tonnes

laden weight nor a passenger vehicle with more than 8 seats –
until the age of 18 when, for example, a public service vehicle
may be driven or a goods vehicle up to 7.5 tonnes laden weight.
Only at the age of 21 can a person have a licence to drive any
vehicle of whatever weight and size.

You are required to have a licence before 'driving' a small
mowing machine or small tractor and this can be obtained from
the age of 16.

Leaflets about driving licences and car registration
requirements are available at post offices and from the Driver
Enquiry Unit, DVLC, Swansea SA6 7JL: *What you need to know
about driver licensing* (D.100) and *Registering and licensing your
motor vehicle . . . some notes to help you* (V.100).

passengers
There are strict regulations about the passenger and driver of a
motor cycle having to wear a crash helmet. If a passenger is
under the age of 16, the person driving the machine will be
held liable for the passenger's contravention of these
regulations.

When a child under the age of 14 is a front seat passenger in a
car, it is the driver's responsibility to see that the child has put
on the safety belt; over the age of 14, the child himself is held
responsible. A child less than one year old must be protected
by being in a specially designed restraint (available for fitting
on to a back seat). There is a Department of Transport leaflet
Child safety in cars which explains the requirements, and the
child restraints that may be fitted.

employment under 18

There are statutory rules governing the conditions under which anyone under the age of 18 may be employed.

Basically, no child under the age of 13 may be employed at all (although this may be permitted by a local authority's byelaw).

Children between the ages of 13 and the end of compulsory school age (this could vary between 15 years 8 months and 16 years 4 months) should not be employed

o during school hours

o before 7 a.m. or after 7 p.m. on any day

o more than two hours on a school day or on a sunday

o to lift move or carry anything so heavy as to be likely to cause injury

o in factories, mines, quarries, construction sites, UK registered ships and certain other undertakings.

There are statutory restrictions which may affect the employment of someone who has left school but is still under 18. For example, the young person may generally not work in any industrial undertaking for more than a maximum number of hours in a day or week, and must not be employed on night work (but the employer may get exemption from such restrictions from the Health and Safety Executive). Certain statutes govern the employment of young people in specific occupations: for example, the Young Persons (Employment) Act 1938 (deliveries, carrying messages and running errands in hotels and places of public entertainment), the Shops Act 1950 and the Factories Act 1961.

Local authorities are empowered under the Children and Young Persons Act 1933 to make byelaws which, amongst other things, permit children under the age of 13 to help parent or guardian with light agricultural or horticultural work, or allow children to be employed in the morning up to one hour before the school day starts – for example, on a paper round. A shop employing children on paper rounds has to be vetted by the local education authority in order to comply with the local byelaws. (A child using his bicycle to deliver newspapers is not covered by the personal liability section of the parents' household contents insurance policy – the parents should make sure that the newsagent's insurance covers this.)

At present, responsibility for enforcing the various regulations is divided between government departments, local authorities, local education authorities, the Health and Safety Executive, the DHSS, the police. There is an Employment of Children Act 1973, tightening up the law relating to child employment by replacing local byelaws with standardising regulations, which has been passed but has not been implemented.

Working Children, pamphlet no 34 published in 1985 by the **Low Pay Unit** (£1.75 from the LPU, 9 Upper Berkeley Street, London W1H 8BY) documents the current law and summarises the present situation, based on a survey of children's employment. The pamphlet concludes that "the regulations that currently exist to protect children at work are patchy and poorly enforced . . . children remain vulnerable despite the complex net of legal regulations".

The **Health and Safety Executive** (HSE) (Baynard's House, 1 Chepstow Place, London W2 4TF, telephone: 01-229 3456) has published a free booklet on safety for young workers *Mind how you go!* and also leaflets, aimed at employers, on the safety aspects of employment of children in agriculture. (Enquiries about HSE publications to St. Hugh's House, Stanley Precinct, Bootle, Merseyside L20 3QY, telephone: 051 951 4381.)

children in entertainment

There are detailed regulations concerning children taking part in entertainment. The basic rule is that with limited exceptions, no child under 16 may take part in a public performance without the employer having obtained a local authority licence if

○ there is to be a charge for admission, or

○ the performance takes place on licensed premises, or

○ it is to be broadcast, or recorded with a view to being broadcast, or made into a film intended for public exhibition.

A licence is not required where the performance takes place at school or church and the child is to receive no payment other than for expenses.

Where the child is under 14, a licence will not be granted unless the child is taking part in an acting role which cannot be performed except by someone of about that age, or the child is performing in a ballet or opera or a mainly musical event.

The local authority will not give a licence unless satisfied of the child's fitness, that proper provision has been made for his health and kind treatment, that his education will not suffer, and that the child's parent or guardian consents. Any parent who allows a child to take part in an unlicensed performance commits an offence and risks a fine or imprisonment.

For a young person who is to perform abroad, a licence has to be granted by magistrates. Such a licence is required for anyone up to 18 years of age.

national insurance

The duty to pay national insurance contributions arises on the 16th birthday, when your national insurance record (leading eventually to a state retirement pension) starts.

You will be sent a 'National Insurance Numbercard', a plastic card with the national insurence number you will have for the rest of your life and your name on it.

If you are not earning, you are credited with contributions up to the 18th birthday. If earning over the age of 16, class 1 national insurance contributions have to be deducted by the employer if the earnings are more than the statutory lower earnings limit (£35.50 a week for 1985/86). If earning less than the lower earnings limit, you do not have to make national insurance contributions – but are not credited with them. Voluntary national insurance contributions (class 3) can be paid to fill a contribution gap.

DHSS leaflet FB20 *Leaving school?* and FB23 *Going to college or university?* are pocket guides to social security, explaining what you pay and what you get.

– claiming
Someone who has left school and who is not in full-time employment is eligible to claim supplementary benefit if his means are less than the statutory scale rate for a single person. (Benefit will not be paid until the first monday in September or January or the one after Easter Monday, whichever comes first after the last school term ended.)

To be entitled to claim, someone under 18 has to register at a local careers advice centre and then sign on at an unemployment benefit office.

Unemployment benefit and sickness benefit are not available until a qualifying number of national insurance contributions have been paid (see DHSS leaflets FB9 *Unemployed? help you can get to make ends meet* and NI12 *Unemployment benefit*).

Statutory sick pay is payable by an employer (unless you are taken on for less than 3 months) depending on the amount you are earning (see DHSS leaflets NI16 *SSP and sickness benefit* and NI244 *Check your right to statutory sick pay*).

Even if you are not claiming supplementary benefit and cannot claim unemployment benefit, it is important to sign on at the unemployment benefit office so that you can be credited with national insurance contributions which will count, eventually, towards your entitlement to unemployment benefit and – a long way ahead – towards your right to receive a state pension on retirement.

child's income

Any child – no matter how young – is taxed on earned and investment income in the same way as an adult. Grants and scholarships do not normally count as income. But money paid under a court order (by a father after the parents have divorced, for example) or deed of covenant counts as income.

The child can claim the single person's personal tax allowance, and any other allowance for which he may qualify. So, a child can have up to the amount of his personal tax allowance (£2,205 in the 1985/86 tax year) of income without paying tax. Inland Revenue leaflet IR22 give details of personal tax allowances.

If tax has been deducted before the child gets the money, the child can, if his income is low enough, claim tax back. In practice, the parent or guardian does this for the child. (The tax deducted from interest paid on a building society or bank deposit account cannot be reclaimed by anyone.)

If parents give an unmarried child of theirs aged under 18 anything which produces investment income, this income, unless it is £5 or less, will normally count as the parents' income, and has to be entered on their tax return. If the parents are divorced or separated, the income counts as that of the parent who makes the gift.

But if the parents set up an 'accumulation trust' for the child, so that the interest is accumulated, not spent, until the child reaches the age of 18 (or marries), the income does not count as the parents'.

The *Which? Book of Tax* includes sections on tax and children, and on trusts and tax.

prohibited purchases

It is against the law for a child (depending on age) to be sold certain commodities. For instance, anyone under the age of 12 must not be allowed to buy a pet, anyone under the age of 16 cannot lawfully be sold fireworks.

tobacco and alcohol
A child under 16 may not be sold tobacco or cigarettes. Even if the child is given them by someone who was entitled to buy them, it is prohibited for young people under 16 to smoke in public. A police officer or park-keeper in uniform may seize cigarettes or tobacco from a person under 16 smoking in a public place.

At 14, a child may go into a pub with an adult but must not be sold intoxicating liquor in a bar or an off-licence under the age of 18. At 16, a child can have an alcoholic drink with a meal in a restaurant, and liqueur chocolates can be bought at the age of 16.

It is illegal to sell to anyone under 18 a substance 'likely to be inhaled . . . for the purpose of causing intoxication' (such as glue). There is a Health Education Council leaflet *What to do about glue sniffing* with advice for parents on the misuse of glue and other solvents.

drugs
It is illegal at any age to traffic in or possess drugs controlled under the Misuse of Drugs Act. Anyone found in possession of such drugs may be prosecuted or cautioned, depending on the severity of the offence and the police force's policy.

Possession of some drugs such as heroin, cocaine and LSD can lead to prison sentences of up to 7 years. Trafficking – that is, importing, distributing, selling, supplying or possessing with intent to supply to others – can lead to life imprisonment. For other drugs, such as amphetamines, barbiturate and cannabis, sentences can range up to 5 years' imprisonment for possession and 14 years for trafficking.

The DHSS pamphlet *What parents can do about drugs* (DM2) gives advice and information for anyone concerned about a teenager's health and wellbeing. It points out that no one risks prosecution by seeking medical help for a drug problem.

The **Institute for the Study of Drug Dependence** (1–4 Hatton Place, Hatton Garden, London EC1N 8ND, telephone: 01-430 1991) has various publications on the non-medical use of drugs, including the leaflets *Drugs: what every parent should know* (70p) and *Drug misuse: a basic briefing* (single copies free), and a book *Sniffing solvents: a new guide for professionals and parents* (£4.50). Information about volunteer groups offering support, and other sources of information and advice for the parents of drug users is available also from the **Standing Conference on Drug Abuse** (same address as ISDD, telephone: 01-430 2341).

firearms

It is illegal to sell or hire an airgun or air pistol and ammunition to a young person under 17, but such a weapon may be given or lent to anyone aged over 14. Anyone who gives an air weapon to a child under 14 is committing an offence and may be fined. The Home Office's leaflet *Gun sense is good sense* is a guide to the safe use of air weapons.

No firearm certificate is needed for air weapons except for certain types which are declared specially dangerous by the Home Office.

But anyone wanting to buy or have any shot gun, rifle, pistol, revolver or specially dangerous air weapon, must first obtain the appropriate certificate from the local chief officer of police.

The Home Office's leaflet *Firearms: what you need to know about the law* says regarding young people:

> **If you are under 14 years of age** you may not possess, purchase or acquire any firearm or ammunition, nor may anyone give or lend you any. But there are the following exceptions to this general rule.
>
> I   You may possess and use firearms and ammunition:
>
>   a   as a member of an approved club: or
>
>   b   when you are shooting in a shooting gallery where only air weapons or miniature rifles are available.
>
> II   You may possess and use any air weapon if you are not in a public place and are using it under the supervision of somebody over 21: but you may not use it for firing a missile beyond the premises or land where you are being supervised.
>
> III   You may carry a firearm or ammunition under the instruction of another person who holds a certificate and for his or her use for sporting purposes only.
>
> **If you are 14 or over** you may be given or lent an air weapon or its ammunition and if you have a firearm certificate, you may be given or lent any firearm or ammunition.
>
> **If you are under 15** and have a shot gun certificate you may have with you an assembled shot gun provided you are supervised by a person over 21 or the shot gun is in a gun cover securely fastened.
>
> **If you are 15 or over** and have a shot gun certificate, you may be given a shot gun as a gift.
>
> **If you are under 17** you may not purchase or hire a firearm or its ammunition.
>
> **If you are under 17** you may carry an air gun or air rifle in a public place, but only if it is in a gun cover securely fastened.

The law treats anyone over the age of 17 as an adult in relation to firearms.

The Home Office leaflets are available at police stations and from citizens advice bureaux.

legal advice

Citizens advice bureaux and legal advice centres give free advice to anyone who goes to them. CAB offices have numerous leaflets and information about local sources of help and services. The address of a local CAB will be in the telephone directory.

The **Children's Legal Centre** (20 Compton Terrace, London N1 2UN, telephone: 01-359 6251) is an independent body concerned with laws and policies which affect children and young people in England and Wales. It provides a free advice and information service on all aspects of the law affecting children, by letter and by telephone (2 p.m. to 5 p.m., monday to friday). The Centre publishes reports, handbooks and information sheets, and a bulletin *Childright* (subscription £18.50 for 10 issues); also a 4-page pull-out *At what age can I . . . ?* (40p).

The **National Council for Civil Liberties** (21 Tabard Street, London SE1 4LA, telephone: 01-403 3888) includes amongst its publications *First Rights*, a practical guide to the rights of, and written for, children and young people (1985 edition £1.95 plus postage).

solicitors

Anyone, child or parent, can go to a solicitor for advice at any time on a dispute arising within the family on legal rights or responsibilities or contracts.

Solicitors in an area are listed, with names of individuals, as well as firms, in the annual *Solicitors' Regional Directory* (kept at reference libraries and CABx) which gives an indication of the categories of work in which they are experienced.

If you do not think you can afford to pay a solicitor's normal charges, ask whether he participates in the 'fixed-fee' interview system, whereby you can get up to a half-hour session with a solicitor for a flat fee of £5. The *Solicitors' Regional Directory* indicates which firms participate in the scheme. Make sure that you tell the solicitor before the session that it is to be 'fixed-fee'.

legal advice ('green form') scheme

If your income is low (or non-existent), ask the solicitor to assess whether you are financially eligible for the statutory legal advice and assistance scheme, colloquially referred to as the 'green form' scheme ('pink form' in Scotland). If so, you can get a solicitor's advice free, or subsidised. The solicitor will need to have details of your income, savings or capital, any dependants, in order to complete the green (or pink) application form. The solicitor can tell you there and then whether or not you qualify and whether you have to pay a contribution based on your income. Not all solicitors take on 'green form' work.

Under the 'green form' scheme, a solicitor can give you advice, write letters and make telephone calls for you, prepare draft statements. The initial limit is £50-worth of his time; this means approximately two hours' work. The scheme does not include the solicitor appearing for you in court. But if you have to take a domestic case to the magistrates' court, the solicitor can apply to the legal aid office to be allowed to 'assist you by way of representation' at the court hearing. (This facility does not exist in Scotland.)

legal aid scheme

To get financial help for a solicitor to represent you in any other civil case, you can apply for a civil legal aid certificate. The local legal aid office will assess the legal merits of your case, and the DHSS will assess your resources to discover whether you are within the financial limits of the scheme (these differ from the financial limits for the 'green form' scheme). If you and your case meet the criteria, you are issued with a legal aid certificate which enables the solicitor from then on to work on your case without charging you. You may be required to make a contribution to the scheme, according to your income and/or capital.

For a criminal case, legal aid has to be applied for through the court dealing with the case. It will only be granted if it is in the interest of justice that you should be legally represented and you need help in paying for it. The court office can supply the necessary forms for applying and for giving details of income and capital or savings, so that your financial eligibility and any contribution required from you can be calculated. (In Scotland, criminal legal aid is applied for through a solicitor, although determined by the court.)

Anyone receiving supplementary benefit or family income supplement can get legal aid without having to make a contribution and may be able to get legal advice under the 'green form' (or 'pink form') scheme if he or she does not have too much capital.

The basic facts about legal aid, including the legal advice scheme, and the current financial limits are given in leaflets issued by the Law Society and available at citizens advice bureaux and other advice agencies.

– for a young person
For someone under the age of 16, an application for legal advice under the 'green form' scheme has generally to be made by the parents. The solicitor can, however, give 'green form' advice to the child direct, provided he has obtained authority from the legal aid area secretary. It is usually the parents' resources that are assessed for financial eligibility but if a child is in care or subject to a 'place of safety' order, he makes the application in his own right and the parent's means are not assessed.

Once the child is 16, he can apply on his own and the financial assessment is made on his means (including any payments or allowance from the parents).

For civil legal aid, the parents have to apply and are assessed financially on the child's behalf while he is under 16; while he is under 18, the parent must also sign the application form. (In Scotland, no counter-signature is necessary once the child is 16.) Once over 16, the child is generally assessed on his own resources.

An application for criminal legal aid for someone under 16 must be signed by a parent, together with a statement of the parent's means. Over the age of 16, the young person may apply and be assessed in his own right although a parent may still apply on the child's behalf while he is under the age of 17.

children and the criminal law

The criminal law makes the distinction between

○ adults – anyone aged 17 or over

and

○ juveniles – anyone aged under 17.

Once a child is 17, he will be dealt with like any other adult offender, in a magistrates' court where the proceedings will be heard in public; for certain more serious offences, such as theft or burglary, he will have a right to elect trial by jury in the crown court. Juveniles do not have this right, whatever the offence charged.

'Juveniles' are sub-divided into

○ 'children' (aged 10 years to 13 years inclusive)

and

○ 'young persons' (aged 14 years to 16 years inclusive).

No child under the age of 10 can be guilty of any offence in law. But a juvenile under 10 committing what would be a criminal offence in an older person can be brought before the court in care proceedings.

A 'child' between his 10th and his 13th birthday may be convicted only if the prosecution proves not only that the child committed the offence but also that he knew at the time that what he was doing was wrong.

which court

Generally speaking, whatever the nature of the offence, a juvenile will be tried in a 'juvenile court', which is a special form of magistrates' court. The hearings are in private, before three magistrates (including at least one man and one woman) drawn from a panel of magistrates specialising in juvenile court work.

The only occasions on which a juvenile may be tried before a different court are

○ where he is charged with homicide or some other very serious offence: such a case will be dealt with by the crown court (he will first appear before the juvenile court to be committed for trial to the crown court)

○ where he is charged jointly with a person aged over 17, in which case he may be tried as an adult before a magistrates' court or the crown court (the adult may be committed there and the juvenile may go with him). Nor is it just joint charges which will keep the adult and juvenile together – it may be aiding, abetting, causing, procuring, allowing or permitting the other's offence.

An adult magistrates' court has only limited powers to sentence a juvenile, so will usually remit him to a juvenile court on finding him guilty. A crown court (which in such a case usually has two juvenile court justices sitting with the judge) will normally itself sentence both the adult and the juvenile.

police and juveniles

Many police forces do not prosecute a juvenile without first referring the case to their juvenile bureau (or youth and community section). Juvenile bureaux are usually staffed by police officers specialising in working with children, who liaise, in some areas very closely, with other relevant agencies such as the social services department, schools, youth groups. They basically act as a filter process in deciding which kids to prosecute and which to caution); some apply more lenient criteria than others.

cautioning

Instead of prosecuting a juvenile, the police may decide to caution him. A police caution is an attempt to keep a young person out of court and from having a criminal record. A criminal record would remain with him for the rest of his life: a record is kept of all convictions at the Criminal Records Office at Scotland Yard.

The caution is an official warning and a record is kept, but only until the person is 17 years old. If he re-offends, that caution will be cited in court whether he was 10 or 16 when the original offence occurred. If he does not re-offend before he is 17, the record of his caution is then destroyed.

Cautioning may entail the child and his parents coming to the police station. The caution may only be given if a parent or guardian is present, consents to the caution, and the juvenile admits the offence. No pressure should be put on the child to agree to a caution. If there is any doubt at all, legal advice should first be sought.

at the police station

The police have identical powers of arrest for juveniles as for adults.

For a juvenile who is arrested and taken to the police station, however, special rules apply. For example:

○ the police must take steps, so far as is practicable, to ensure that the parents or guardian are informed of the juvenile's arrest, or the person currently responsible for his welfare (where there is a supervision order, the person responsible for supervision has to be informed, or the local authority if the child is in care)

○ so far as is practicable, the police should not question him unless his parent or guardian or some other adult responsible for him is present

○ if a juvenile makes a written statement, this should be done in the presence of his parent or guardian or some other non-involved adult who is not a police officer and is of the same sex as the child, who should also sign the statement as witness.

From 1 January 1986, codes of practice under the Police and Criminal Evidence Act 1984 must be followed by the police regarding their powers and duties in connection with anyone brought to a police station. The codes deal with detention, treatment and questioning, and identification (including finger-prints, photographs, body searches and samples) by police officers. There are special provisions for the treatment of juveniles – for example, relating to the 'appropriate adult' to be with them, legal advice, interviews, making statements, being cautioned, put into care, being charged.

These codes must be available and shown to anyone coming to a police station, voluntarily or after being brought there by the police.

A parent, when called to the police station, should be careful not to put pressure on the child to admit to committing an offence. The basic rule is that he is not obliged to say anything at all in answer to any charge and the parent should ensure that the child is clear on this. He is also entitled, as is any person in detention, to consult a solicitor and to see the solicitor in private.

If the juvenile needs legal advice while at a police station, or for a first appearance in court on a criminal charge, he can ask to see the duty solicitor who will provide advice and initial representation, usually free of charge.

It may be decided there and then to take no further action and to release the juvenile from the police station without bringing a charge. The case may be referred to the juvenile bureau before deciding how to deal with it.

The police may, however, keep the juvenile in cusotdy but must then bring him before the court within 36 hours. He should not be kept in a police cell meanwhile but should be transferred to the care of the local authority.

– remanding

In a very serious case, the juvenile court may decide that the juvenile should be remanded in care pending trial. This means that he is placed into the care of the local authority and may be kept in a community home pending the hearing.

If charged with homicide or other serious offence, or where a boy aged 15 or 16 is so unruly that he cannot safely be committed to the care of a local authority, he can be placed in a remand centre (in practical terms, not very different from prison) or sent to an adult prison if there is no vacancy at the remand centre. (Girls of 15 or 16 cannot be sent to a remand centre.)

the hearing

Juvenile court proceedings are kept separate from adult proceedings in the magistrates' court. It is an offence for a newspaper report to publish any details calculated to lead to the identification of any child or young person concerned in proceedings in a juvenile court except where specifically authorised so as to avoid injustice to the juvenile.

The procedure in a juvenile court tends to be less formal than in other courts. The child's parents or guardian will normally be required to attend and may represent their child if he does not have a legal representative.

Magistrates usually sit behind a table on the same level and witnesses do not have to "swear by almighty God to tell the truth the whole truth and nothing but the truth" but merely "promise" to do so. Even though some juvenile courts ignore formalities, they are considering the grave issue whether or not the juvenile has committed a criminal offence.

The prosecution has to prove guilt beyond reasonable doubt. If the child is under 14, there is the additional requirement of proving 'knowledge' – that he knew that what he was doing was seriously wrong.

It may be tempting for parents to encourage their child to plead guilty 'to get the case over with'. A parent should never do this. Once a child has got a criminal record, there is the danger that his 'criminal' behaviour will become a self-fulfilling prophecy. The child should be advised to plead guilty only if he clearly committed the offence and knew that it was wrong – the parent may not be the best person to judge this. If there is any doubt, seek legal advice.

sentence

A juvenile who is found guilty (the term 'convicted' is not used in respect of juveniles) will not be sent to prison. No person under the age of 21 may be sentenced to imprisonment.

The following possible sentences (also referred to as 'disposals') may be imposed for offences that in the case of an adult are punishable with imprisonment:

○ **youth custody** (age 15 to 20 inclusive)
This sentence means being kept in a youth custody centre for more than 4 months. For someone under 17, the maximum is 12 months. For someone aged 17 or over, it is up to the maximum sentence for which someone over 21 could be imprisoned: for example, maximum of 10 years for theft, 14 years for burglary.

Youth custody is a sentence for an offender "unable or unwilling to respond to non-custodial penalties or because a custodial sentence is necessary for the protection of the public or because the offence was so serious that a non-custodial sentence cannot be justified".

○ **detention centre** (male offenders only, age 14 to 20 inclusive)
This 'short sharp shock' is used where the court is of the view that a custodial sentence of no more than 4 months is appropriate. The regime at detention centres concentrates on military-style discipline and physical exercise.

○ **community service order** (age 16 and over)
The offender is required to participate in a community project supervised by a probation officer. He will be required to carry out unpaid work within the following 12 months, up to a maximum of 120 hours for someone aged between 16 and 17 (maximum 240 hours if older); the minimum number of hours is 40.

If the offender fails to carry out the required work (that is, he is in breach of the order), the probation officer may apply to revoke it and the offender will become liable to be sentenced for the original offence again.

○ **attendance centre**
The offender is required to take part in supervised activities (such as physical drill or craft work) at an attendance centre. The maximum number of hours required is between 12 and 24 or 36, depending on age, with not more than 2 or 3 hours on any one day.

These centres are run by Home Office nominees who in some cases are police officers, or may be probation officers, school teachers, prison officers working privately (that is, not in their professional capacities). This sentence can only be imposed if there is an attendance centre available; it is often used as a way of dealing with football hooligans.

○ **care order**
For an offender aged under 17 who is in need of care or control which he is unlikely otherwise to receive, the magistrates have the power to make a care order. This means that the juvenile will be taken into local authority care, possibly until he is 18 (until 19 if he was 16 when the order was made).

For offences for which an adult would be either sent to prison or fined, a juvenile court may imposed the following:

○ **supervision order**
A juvenile may be placed under the supervision of the local authority (in practice, usually a social worker) or a probation officer if the offender is over 17, for up to three years. The terms of the order may include 'intermediate treatment' (organised group activities) or a stipulated activity or a 'refraining order' prohibiting participation in specified activities.

If the juvenile fails to comply with the terms of the supervision order laid down by the magistrates or if he does not cooperate with the social worker, the social worker may apply to the magistrates. When dealing with a breach of supervision, the court may fine the offender or make an attendance centre order; or discharge the supervision order and make a care order instead.

○ **fine**
The maximum fine for anyone under the age of 14 is £100;
for someone over 14 and under 17, the maximum is £400.

○ **compensation order**
As an alternative or in addition to imposing a fine or any
other sentence, the magistrates may require the juvenile to
pay compensation to the victim up to a maximum of £2000.

Wherever the court considers a fine or a compensation order
to be appropriate, the parent or guardian will be ordered to
pay instead of the juvenile unless the parent or guardian
cannot be found or the court considers it would be
unreasonable to make such an order because the parent had
not conduced to the offence.

When finding guilty of a relatively small offence, magistrates
may decide not to impose a penalty but to give an absolute or
conditional discharge.

An absolute discharge is a decision that no penalty be applied
(but the finding of guilt is recorded). A conditional discharge
is a decision that, provided no other offence is committed in
the stated time (up to 3 years), no penalty will be imposed.

Alternatively, the magistrates may 'bind over' the offender,
who has to sign an undertaking that he will be of good
behaviour for up to a specified period; if he defaults, he has to
pay an amount stated in the undertaking.

The court may also require the parents 'to enter into a
recognizance' to take proper care and exercise proper control of
the child, for up to 3 years for an amount of up to £1000 on
default.

The magistrates may, with the offender's consent, defer
passing sentence for up to six months and then determine what
the sentence shall be in the light of the offender's conduct
during that period.

An information sheet *Going to court – a young person's guide to
the juvenile court* (40p) is available from the Children's Legal
Centre (20 Compton Terrace, London N1 2UN).

The Cobden Trust's booklet *In whose best interests? the unjust treatment of children in courts and institutions* (£2.50 plus 40p postage) was published in 1980. Amongst publications available from the National Council for Civil Liberties (NCCL) are fact sheets *Know your rights* (£1.50 the set plus 25p postage) which include ones on arrest, police questioning, searches; also booklets on policing and criminal procedure. Cobden Trust and NCCL publications are available from 21 Tabard Street, London SE1 4LA.

in Scotland: children's hearings

The unique 'children's hearing' system in Scotland has a jurisdiction wider than the juvenile courts in England and provides an informal forum for parents to discuss the needs of their child when the child has been identified as in need of care or control.

The reporter to the children's hearing panel is the key official in the operation of the system of juvenile justice. His basic task is to decide whether or not the children who are referred to him should be brought before the panel.

A child must be brought before the panel if it appears that the child is in need of some compulsory measures of care. 'Care' includes protection, control, guidance and treatment. These terms are sufficiently wide for many children to be referred who would not normally come to the attention of the authorities: a child having committed an offence is only one of the eight separate conditions which may justify referral.

Cases involving criminal offences are normally referred to a children's hearing by the police or procurator fiscal but many referrals are made by social workers, headteachers, health visitors, doctors and youth workers.

The parents are kept fully advised and are expected to attend when their child is before the panel in order that the child's whole needs and behaviour can be discussed with a view to deciding on the appropriate action for the child.

The panel consists of three lay members, at least one of whom must be a woman. The reporter presents the case with the necessary background reports on the child. The case is presented informally and in private; the participants normally sit round a large table in the style of a meeting, with a chairman. The panel has wide powers of disposal, and any supervision requirements are reviewed periodically by the panel.

Any appearance before the children's hearing will not be regarded as a criminal record but may be referred to.

in court
If the child does not admit the grounds of referral and disputes that they are an accurate summary of his behaviour or circumstances, the case will be remitted for a hearing before the sheriff to try and establish the grounds of referral in much the same way as an accused may be brought to trial. The case is still presented by the reporter and the child may seek legal representation for this part of the procedure.

In the case of a serious offence, the child will not be referred to the reporter but will be tried in the same way as an adult. A child, however, will not be obliged to swear an oath and can elect to make a statement to the court, which will not be subject to cross-examination, instead of giving evidence. Significantly, the court may still remit the case to a reporter to seek the advice of the children's hearing or may remit the case to a hearing for disposal. It is of the essence of the system that all cases involving children are dealt with as speedily as possible.

ages
A child under the age of eight cannot be subject to criminal prosecution although he or she may still require compulsory measures of care, or control. A child attains the age of criminal responsibility at the age of eight in Scotland. It is assumed that children of eight years and above have developed a moral sense of right and wrong.

In general, children over the age of sixteen are dealt with by the courts. The range of disposals available to the court for children between the ages of sixteen and eighteen is similar to that in England.

The Scottish Education Department's Social Work Services Group has published a brief guide to the scottish system called *Children's Hearings* available from HMSO (£3.80).

when your child is injured

In certain circumstances, damages may be claimed for injuries a child has received.

The basic rule in any claim is that, in order to be able to recover damages, you must prove that the injury was caused by someone else's negligence. Broadly, this means proving that the care used by the person causing the injury did not come up to the standard of reasonable care that might be expected from a person carrying out that activity.

The possibility of suing for damages on behalf of a child could arise in a variety of situations where the defendant is likely to be covered by insurance and could therefore be worth suing.

at school

Children may be injured at school – for example, by defective equipment in the gym, as a result of inadequately supervised sporting activity or, if they are very young, being allowed to wander off unsupervised and get themselves hurt. Schools are not expected to be perfect and they will be judged by the standard of care of the reasonably competent parent.

The local education authority (or in an independent school, the owners of the establishment) will be liable for the negligence of its teachers provided the teacher was acting in the course of his or her employment. If you succeed in obtaining damages against the school employing the teacher, it is their insurers who are likely to pay up on the judgment.

Registered childminders have to accept responsibility for injuries to children in their care and for damage caused by a child in their care to other people or their property. There is a special public liability insurance for members of the National Childminding Association.

Foster parents have been held not to be agents of the local authority and to be personally liable in the case of injury to a child in their care. But they can themselves take out insurance to cover their liability.

by a motorist

All motorists (including learner drivers) must be insured against their liability for causing death or personal injury to other road users including their passengers. But the insurance company is only liable to pay out if it can be shown that their insured was in some way at fault. If you can establish negligence when your child has been injured in a road traffic accident, you know that there is some point in suing because the motorist's insurers will pay the damages awarded. Where a driver was not insured at all or, as in the case of a hit-and-run incident, cannot be traced, the claim would be paid by the Motor Insurers' Bureau (The New Garden House, 78 Hatton Garden, London EC1N 8JQ).

Where your child is a passenger in a car being driven by you and you are involved in an accident, the child has a right to sue you and may recover damages against you provided it can be shown that you were guilty of some negligence, however minimal. A child passenger cannot be held contributorily negligent and therefore if he can prove even 1% of negligence against anyone (driver of the vehicle or third party) he will recover damages in full.

doctors and hospital

Surgical treatment of a child under the age of 16 (in Scotland, a boy under 15, girl under 13) requires the parent's consent.

Consenting to an operation does not mean that you are also consenting to any injury suffered as a result of a negligently performed operation or negligently administered treatment. It is important in cases of doubt that parents should specifically ask the doctor about any possible risks inherent in the proposed way of treating or not treating the child.

In a medical negligence claim, proving negligence is often very difficult because it is not enough to show that the operation or treatment has 'gone wrong'. You would have to prove that someone involved in the treatment of the patient fell short of the standards of the reasonably competent doctor or surgeon on the basis of medical knowledge generally available at the time and that this caused your child's injury or disability.

vaccine damage
Under the Vaccine Damage Payments Act 1979, anyone severely disabled as a result of

o a vaccination given to him

o a vaccination given to his mother before he was born

o having contracted the disease from a person to whom a vaccination was given

is entitled to claim a lump sum payment of £20,000. This sum may be claimed whether or not any person concerned with the administering of the injection was negligent. (Claiming this does not pre-empt the right to sue for damages. But where such a claim for negligence is successful, the statutory amount will be deducted from any damages that are recovered.)

A claim cannot be made until the child has reached the age of two, and must be made within 6 years of either the vaccination or the child's second birthday. The claim for anyone under the age of 18 must be made by the parent or guardian.

Claim forms may be obtained from: Vaccine Damage Payments Unit, Department of Health and Social Security, North Fylde Central Offices, Norcross, Blackpool FY5 3TA. See also DHSS leaflet HB3 *Payment for severe vaccine damage.*

by an animal

If your child is injured by an animal not commonly domesticated in this country, the keeper of the animal is liable even if he has not been negligent at all. With animals commonly domesticated in this country (for example, dogs and horses), someone injured by the animal will normally only be able to sue if negligence can be proved – for example, failure of the rider to control a horse while using the road.

If you can prove that the animal was unusually prone to cause injury and that the keeper specifically knew or ought to have known of this, he will be liable without your having to prove that he was negligent. If the animal belongs to a child under the age of 16, the 'keeper' of the animal who is held responsible is the head of the household of which the child is a member.

dangerous premises

Like anyone else, if a child is on somebody else's premises where he is a 'lawful visitor', he is owed what is known as the 'common duty of care': basically, the occupier must ensure that the premises are reasonably safe for the purpose for which the visitor is there. If the premises are occupied for business purposes, the occupier cannot exclude his liability for causing death or personal injury.

The Occupier's Liability Act 1984 puts the occupier (person or body) of premises under a duty also to trespassers in respect of any risk of injury caused by the state of the premises if

○ he is aware of the danger or has reasonable grounds to believe that it exists

○ he has reasonable grounds to believe that a trespasser may come into the vicinity of the danger concerned

○ the risk is one against which in all the circumstances he should reasonably be expected to offer some protection.

This is particularly relevant if a child wanders off somewhere where he is not supposed to go.

It is likely that in the case of children, a warning notice may not in itself be sufficient to exempt the occupier or owner from liability. Each case would depend on its own facts, including the age of the child and the nature of the danger. Where the child is very young, however, an occupier may be able to escape liability if it can be shown that the person mainly to blame was, in fact, the parent for not having kept a proper eye on the child.

contributory negligence

Damages may be reduced if the person being sued can prove what is known as 'contributory negligence' – that is, that the child should have taken more care of his own safety. The child will not, however, be judged by the standards that would apply to an adult but by those of a reasonable child of that age. If the parent was at fault, any damages the person being sued is ordered to pay may be reduced in proportion to the parent's share of responsibility.

bringing a claim

Suing for damages is a specialised business and should not be undertaken without expert legal advice.

A claim is brought in the High Court if the damages are likely to exceed £5,000, in the county court if they are not likely to exceed £3,000. If the likely damages are between £3,000 and £5,000, you have a choice of which court to apply to.

A person under 18 cannot sue in his own name but needs to sue through an adult, known as a 'next friend'. One or other parent can apply to the court to be appointed next friend, in order to bring the proceedings on the child's behalf. If proceedings are commenced in the High Court, the next friend signs a written form of consent (there is no prescribed form for this) and the solicitor signs a statement that so far as he is aware the plaintiff is under 18 and that there is no conflict of interests between the child and the next friend. In the county court, the next friend merely signs a form saying that he consents to act and undertakes to be responsible for the child's costs.

The limitation period on claiming for personal injury is three years, but for a child this does not start to run until he reaches 18. The 'child' then has 3 years from his 18th birthday in which to commence proceedings if these have not already been brought. So, a child who is injured at the age of two, may have another 19 years in which to bring a claim.

what damages can be recovered

Damages for personal injuries are divided into 'pecuniary' (that is actual financial loss such as loss of wages or reduction of earning capacity) and 'non-pecuniary' loss (that is reduction of the enjoyment of life). Pecuniary loss can be more or less calculable; non-pecuniary loss, although not financial, is attributed a price tag for the purposes of assessing damages. (Such a price tag may seem very arbitrary.)

A plaintiff can claim non-pecuniary loss for

○ pain and suffering caused by the injury itself or any operation (it cannot be claimed for periods during which the plaintiff was unconscious)

○ loss of amenity – that is, the extent to which his injuries deprive him of the ability to lead a full life. The more serious the disability and the more it diminishes the quality of life, the higher the amount will be. (Somewhat paradoxically, this can be claimed even while the plaintiff is unconscious for a long time.)

In the case of a child, the pecuniary loss that can normally be claimed is

○ loss of future earnings

There can be a claim for this if the child's injury deprives him of the ability to take paid work of the kind he would otherwise have done. It is a very difficult calculation to make – the basic formula is to calculate the person's potential net pay and then to apply a 'multiplier' to reach a lump sum figure.

○ medical and other expenses

The cost of private medical treatment (for instance, if the child needs cosmetic plastic surgery) can be claimed and also the cost of nursing services where the child is severely disabled. If one of the family gives up work to look after a severely disabled child, the commercial cost of this can be included.

If you settle for a figure or are awarded damages at the time and the injuries subsequently turn out to be worse than was expected, it is possible in certain circumstances to go back for a further award in the event of serious disease or deterioration in physical or medical condition arising in the future.

Any out-of-court settlement on behalf of a child under 18 must be approved by the court if it is to be binding. Or, if the court's approval is not sought for an out-of-court settlement, the parents will be asked to sign an indemnity form so that if when the child grows up he re-opens the case the insurance company can go against the parents for any additional sums it has had to pay out.

Any payment in damages which a child is awarded by the court will remain in the control of the court until he reaches the age of 18. The court will invest the money on the child's behalf. It is, however, possible to apply to the court for sums to be paid out for specified purposes.

in Scotland

The plaintiff is known as the 'pursuer' in the action. It is usual for a person under the age of eighteen to have a curator *ad litem* appointed by the court to act on his behalf or assist in the litigation. The curator *ad litem* is normally a parent, guardian or independent solicitor.

Claims of any size above £1000 may be pursued by way of an ordinary action in the sheriff court or the court of session. Claims for less than £1000 must be raised by way of summary cause action for payment in the sheriff court. It may not be necessary to use the services of a solicitor for this type of action although it is usual to do so, and legal aid is available.

payment from the state

If your child is severely disabled, physically or mentally, through illness or injury as the result of an accident, you may be able to claim through the DHSS

○ **attendance allowance**
available for children aged 2 or over who require substantially more attention or supervision than is normal for a child of that age and sex
see DHSS leaflet NI205

○ **invalid care allowance**
for anyone who has to stay home to look after the child (but not if you are the woman of a couple – married or unmarried, or separated and getting maintenance equal to or more than the amount of the invalid care allowance)
see DHSS leaflet NI212

○ **mobility allowance**
for a child aged 5 or over who is incapable of walking or virtually unable to walk
see DHSS leaflet NI211.

Sums received on the child's behalf by way of mobility or attendance allowance are not taken into account when any damages are awarded for a claim on behalf of the child. They are also ignored when assessing entitlement to supplementary benefit. These DHSS benefits are payable whether or not the injuries were due to someone else's fault, unlike damages which are only recoverable if fault can be established.

if child is killed

If a child is killed due to a third party's negligence, the damages that are likely to be recoverable are far lower than where the child does not die but is severely injured. The essential crux of damages is compensation for actual measurable loss. Bereaved parents are often shocked and outraged to find how little value the law seems to place on the life of a dead child.

There are basically two courses of action, both of which depend on being able to prove that somebody was negligent.

– on the child's behalf

The child's right to sue for damages for his personal injuries does not cease on his death. The action may be brought on behalf of his estate but the damages will rarely amount to a great deal. There will be no claim for loss of future earnings; the only claim will be for the pain and suffering and loss of amenity while he lived. If death was virtually instantaneous, the damages will be very small.

– action by dependants

His mother and father (mother only if he was illegitimate) may bring an action for damages for bereavement or mental distress. At present, a sum of £3,500 is payable in respect of such a claim; if both parents claim, it is shared between them. (In Scotland, the amount is at the court's discretion.)

Over and above this, parents may claim for any pecuniary loss that they have suffered as a result of the child's death. In practice they will normally recover nothing. But if the child was already in work or training for a profession and it could be shown that the parents had a reasonable expectation of receiving some pecuniary advantage from the child's employment or future employment, they could claim damages against the person or body whose default caused the death.

if child injures somebody

There is no general basis on which parents are liable for the negligence of their children.

A child's 'negligence' will be judged against the standard of care of a reasonable child of that age. Although someone under the age of 18 can be sued for damages, the practical disincentive is that he will not usually have any money. One obvious exception would be a child of 17 who has injured somebody while driving a car or riding a motor bike. In practice, because of compulsory insurance, such a case would not differ from one where a claim is brought against an adult. It is no defence for a motorist to say that he is a learner driver: he will be judged against the standard of the reasonably competent motorist.

Under the age of 18 a person cannot be sued in his own name but must be represented by a guardian *ad litem*. Usually the court appoints a parent to be guardian *ad litem*, who conducts the action on the child's behalf and instructs a solicitor.

– parent responsible?

A more difficult question is whether a parent can be personally liable for damage caused by a child due to the parent's negligent failure to supervise the child properly. There have been apparently similar cases decided differently where parents have given their child a gun without adequate instructions on how to use it or prohibition about where to fire it. Each case is considered on its facts. The relevant factors will be the age of the child, the dangerousness of the activity, any instructions or other protective steps taken by the parent, whether or not the parent knew the child was disobedient.

If your child is injured by another child, it is possible to claim compensation from the parent of that child but only if it can be shown that the parent had been negligent in failing to supervise the child.

child abused in the family

Parents are liable to prosecution for a number of offences against children listed in the Children and Young Persons Act 1933 under the heading of prevention of cruelty and exposure to moral and physical danger, namely:

"If any person who has attained the age of sixteen years and has the custody, charge, or care of any child or young person under that age, wilfully assaults, ill-treats, neglects, abandons, or exposes him, or causes or procures him to be assaulted, ill-treated, neglected, abandoned, or exposed, in a manner likely to cause him unnecessary suffering or injury to health (including injury to or loss of sight, or hearing, or limb, or organ of the body, and any mental derangement), that person shall be guilty . . ."

duty to alert
The local authority has the responsibility to make enquiries into incidents of apparent or alleged abuse and can take proceedings to bring a child into care. The police and the NSPCC also have powers to institute care proceedings.

A doctor in the course of routine examination of a child may see signs of non-accidental injury. Any person who stands *in loco parentis* to a child and considers the child to need medical treatment as a result of injury is under a duty of care to get the child medically examined and treated.

Anyone – neighbour, friend, relative – can and should tell the NSPCC, the social services department or the police about any situation where there is reason to suspect that a child is being ill treated, neglected or abused.

Increasing awareness of the problem may result in cases of parents having to refute an unfounded accusation of harming their child.

child abuse register

Local authorities are required to establish and keep child abuse registers for children up to the age of 17. The main purposes of a register (which is confidential) are

○ to provide detailed, accessible information about children who are known or suspected to have suffered abuse

○ to provide an aid to the diagnosis of repeated injury or events which might otherwise be seen as unrelated and not identified as a pattern of abuse

○ to open up communication between concerned agencies in the area and avoid duplication of services

○ to provide a basis of regular monitoring of a child and family.

what is 'child abuse'?
The definition of behaviour viewed as abusive has broadened from the original 'battered baby syndrome' and encompasses neglect and emotional abuse.

Although there is no comprehensive definition of the term child abuse the DHSS has recommended certain criteria for the child abuse register:

○ **physical injury**
all physically injured children where the nature of the injury is not consistent with the account of how it occurred, or where there is definite knowledge, or reasonable suspicion, that the injury was inflicted (or knowingly not prevented) by any person having custody, charge or care of the child

○ **physical neglect**
children who have been persistently or severely neglected physically or exposed to dangers, including cold and starvation

○ **emotional abuse**
children who have been medically diagnosed as suffering
from severe failure to thrive for no organic reason, or whose
behaviour and emotional development have been severely
affected, or where medical and social assessments have
found evidence of other persistent or severe neglect or
rejection

○ **previous abuse**
children who are in a household with, or which is regularly
visited by, a parent or another person who has abused a
child, and who are considered at risk of abuse.

Some child abuse registers include sexual abuse as a criterion
for registration. There is no standard view of the types of sexual
behaviour which should be regarded as 'abusive' for child
abuse registration purposes. Two definitions of sexual abuse
are

". . . the involvement of children under 17 in sexual
activities which are intended to gratify adult sexual need."
". . . involving dependent, emotionally immature children
and adolescents in sexual activities they do not truly
comprehend, to which they are unable to given informed
consent, or that violate the social taboos of family roles."

investigation
Diagnosis of child abuse normally requires both medical
examination of the child and social assessment of the family
background. In cases of suspected child abuse, the parents may
be asked to attend the medical examination of the child, but
this is not a legal requirement.

Investigation of a suspected case of child abuse is normally
undertaken by the social services department or the NSPCC, or
in some cases by the police. There will be a case conference
attended by those who have investigated the case, workers
from the social services, health authority and other agencies
who know the family, and the police, to decide whether action

is necessary. When a child's name has been put on the child abuse register, a system for monitoring and reviewing the case should be set up and normally a 'key worker' is made responsible for co-ordinating information on the case.

Parents are not automatically asked to a child abuse case conference, although increasingly it is the practice for parents to be invited to attend part, if not all, of the conference. There is no legal requirement to inform parents that their child's name is placed on the child abuse register, but generally, unless there are exceptional circumstances, parents are informed of the fact of registration. Parents have no statutory right of appeal against the inclusion of their child's name on the register.

The **National Society for the Prevention of Cruelty to Children** (**NSPCC**) (head office: 67 Saffron Hill, London EC1N 8RS, telephone: 01-242 1626)
can give information and advice about child abuse. There are local offices of the NSPCC throughout England, Wales and Northern Ireland (addresses and numbers in the telephone directory).

In Scotland, the head office of the **Royal Scottish Society for the Prevention of Cruelty to Children** is at Melville House, 41 Polwarth Terrace, Edinburgh EH11 1NU, telephone: 031-337 8539.

The **Child Assault Prevention Programme** (30 Windsor Court, Moscow Road, London W2 4SN) offers help and support particularly to children in cases of sexual abuse. *Preventing child sexual assault, a practical guide to talking with children* (£2.80) is available from CAPP.

Parents under strain who feel there is a danger to their child should seek the help of a social worker at the social services department or the NSPCC before thing go too far.

OPUS (Organisations for Parents under Stress) has a 24-hour crisis telephone number 01-645 0505, which can be used by parents who are afraid they may be tempted to harm their children.

on a parent's death

If one parent dies, the children normally go on being looked after by the surviving parent only. If both parents die or the only or surviving parent dies, relatives (for example, grandparents) may bring the child up without any formality or court order being made.

If there is no one willing to act, the local authority is under a duty to take the child into care.

The deceased parent may have appointed a guardian.

guardianship

Guardianship effectively vests all parental rights and duties in the person who is guardian. It differs fundamentally from adoption in that the guardian can be removed by order of the court.

A guardian is trustee of the ward's property and has to account to the ward (the beneficiary) when the guardianship comes to an end.

Anyone who accepts the role of guardian cannot later withdraw; guardianship ceases when the ward reaches the age of 18 or marries.

– appointed by parent

Each parent may appoint, by will or by deed, one or more guardians to act after his or her death or the death of the other parent. A testamentary guardian acts jointly with the surviving parent. If that parent objects, the guardian may apply to the court for a decision.

If each parent has appointed a different guardian, the two guardians act jointly after the second parent dies.

– appointed by the court

A person may be appointed as guardian by the court where either or both of the child's parents are dead and there is no one to look after the child, to act either jointly with or in substitution for the surviving parent.

Any person may apply to the High Court, county court or a magistrates' court to be appointed guardian if

○ there is no parent, guardian or other person having parental rights with respect to the child; *or*

○ the parent has died without appointing a testamentary guardian; *or*

○ any guardian or guardians appointed have refused to act.

Where a child has been orphaned with no testamentary guardian appointed and the child's relatives wish to bring the child up, they may choose to apply for guardianship with its wider powers rather than custodianship, but there is no obligation to apply for either.

Someone who takes an orphan into his or her family and who is entitled to child benefit for the child can claim from the DHSS a weekly (tax-free) payment, called guardian's allowance. This can in some circumstances be paid even if one of the parents is still alive. The conditions and procedure for claiming are given in DHSS leaflet NI14.

parents' wills or intestacy

It is always advisable for a parent to make a will. As well as appointing a guardian, you may also appoint trustees to administer your property after your death on behalf of the children until the children reach a specified age. Guidance on the making of a will is given in the Consumer Publication *Wills and probate*, which also explains what happens where there is no will (intestacy). For example, under the intestacy rules, where there is no surviving spouse, the whole of the estate will be kept on trust for such of the deceased's children as reach the age of 18 (or marry, if younger). In the meantime, they are entitled to be maintained out of the income.

Any reference in a will to 'legitimate children' (or indeed 'my children') includes an adopted child even if the will was made prior to the date of adoption. However, if any disposition depends on the relative seniority of children, an adopted child is treated for this purpose as if born at the date of adoption. On the other hand, if the will speaks of 'all my children who shall reach the age of 18', for that purpose, the adopted child's actual date of birth is the relevant one.

If the parents divorce, this will not affect any will made by either of them in so far as it provides for their children. If, however, either of the parents marries again, that new marriage automatically revokes his or her will. If the remarried parent then dies without having made another will, the children are entitled to share in the intestacy along with any children of the subsequent marriage, after the surviving spouse's share.

if disinherited
Where a remarried parent made a will excluding the children from the previous marriage, on that parent's death, an application may be made under the Inheritance (Provision for Family and Dependants) Act 1975 for maintenance of those children out of the estate. This should be done within 6 months of probate being granted.

The category of child who can apply for provision out of the estate is considerably wider than just the deceased's legitimate children. The following children (amongst other people) may apply to the court on the grounds that the deceased's will or intestacy (or a combination of both) has failed to make reasonable financial provision

○ a child (including illegitimate, legitimated or adopted child)

○ a child in the womb at the time of the deceased's death

○ a child treated as a child of the family relating to any marriages of the deceased.

The court has power to order such provision to be made out of the parent's estate as would be reasonable for the child's maintenance. This includes not only periodical payments but also a lump sum or transfer of property under trust.

parent killed by another's fault

Where a parent is killed due to another's fault, his or her children (including adopted children, stepchildren and illegitimate children) may make a claim against the person who caused the death, under the Fatal Accidents Act 1976.

Any child may sue the wrongdoer to recover the estimated pecuniary loss suffered as a result of the parent's death. The executor should make the claim, but if this is not done within 6 months of the death, the dependants bring one action on behalf of all of them (there may be a claim by a surviving spouse as well). The court estimates what financial benefit each dependant would have received from the relationship if the deceased had lived. This includes the loss of financial benefit where it is the breadwinner who has been killed and loss arising from the death of the parent who had the child's day-to-day care. The child's right to damages will not be reduced by any benefit he or she receives through the deceased's estate or otherwise, such as from a life insurance policy.

child reaches age of

can then

claim personal tax allowance
travel by air at 10% of adult fare

3 weeks   Scotland: have passport
6 weeks   have passport
19 weeks be adopted

2 years
3 years
5 years   be given alcohol to drink at home

must now

be liable to tax

Scotland: have had birth registered
have had birth registered

pay child's air fare
in some areas, pay child's bus fare
cease to get free milk and vitamins
go to school/start full-time education
pay child's fare on trains, buses and
most tubes

7 years	draw money from bank account or building society account, without needing parent's signature
8 years	Scotland: be prosecuted
10 years	be prosecuted in juvenile court
12 years	buy a pet have life insurance policy Scotland: (girl) have some contractual capacity, consent to medical treatment	pay full air fare
13 years	get part-time job
14 years	be sentenced as 'young person' in juvenile court (not in Scotland) go into (but not buy drink in) a pub if with adult	in some areas, pay full fare on buses; have photocard to pay half-fare for London Regional Transport be responsible for wearing seat belt in car

child reaches age of	can then	must now
14 years	(boy) be sentenced to detention centre	
	Scotland: (boy) have some contractual capacity, consent to medical treatment	
	be given or lent air weapon; be given or lent any firearm but must have firearm certificate	
	(boy) be found guilty of rape or unlawful sexual intercourse	
		in some areas, pay full fare on buses
15 years	be sentenced to youth custody centre	
	open Girobank account (with guarantor)	
	see category 15 films	
16 years	leave school	pay for NHS prescriptions
	buy fireworks	pay for NHS dentures (unless in full-time education)
	buy own premium bonds	pay for glasses (unless in full-time education)
	hold licence to drive moped or motorcycle under 50 cc	pay national insurance contributions (unless still being educated)
	drive small mowing machine	be asked for consent to surgical or dental treatment
	take part in public performances for payment in UK without needing licence	no longer travel on parent's passport
	be sent out to beg	pay full fare on trains, tubes and buses
	sign deed poll for change of name	be responsible for wearing crash helmet when passenger on motorcycle
	get married, with parents' consent (Scotland: no consent needed)	
	(girl) have sexual intercourse lawfully	

apply for own passport (with parental consent)

claim supplementary benefit

choose own domicile

go into pub without adult, but not buy alcoholic drink

be assessed on own resources for legal advice scheme, and for legal aid (but parent's signature required on application for civil legal aid)

(boy) join armed forces, with parental consent ($16\frac{1}{2}$ for army and RAF)

buy cigarettes and tobacco and smoke in a public place

have alcoholic drink with a meal in restaurant

be sentenced to community service

not be taken into local authority care

put name on electoral register

17 years

hold driving licence

be prosecuted and sentenced as an adult in magistrates' court

become a street trader

be put on probation

buy or hire any firearm (but must have firearm certificate)

(girl) join armed forces, with parental consent ($17\frac{1}{2}$ for WRAAC)

hold pilot's licence to fly private plane

child reaches age of	can then	must now
18 years	without parental signature: get married apply for legal aid apply for own passport join armed forces	pay for NHS dental treatment (unless full-time student or pregnant) no longer be a ward of court no longer be in local authority care (unless 16 when care order made) no longer be credited with national insurance contributions even if still in full-time education
	enter into any contract	
	vote	
	be liable for debt	
	own property directly (i.e. buy a house)	
	buy alcohol, and drink on public premises	
	pawn an article	
	serve on jury	
	make a will	
	work behind bar serving drinks	
	place bet in betting shop	
	partake in bingo session	
	be tattooed	
	be a blood donor	
	go into sex shop	
	buy video recording with R.18 adult classification	

21 years

see category 18 films

(if adopted) apply to Registrar General to get original birth certificate

be sent to prison

become member of parliament or local councillor

apply for licence to sell alcohol

adopt a child

consent to homosexual act (if in private and partner also over 21)

hold licence to drive vehicle with more than 8 passenger seats

index

166 *index*

consumer publications

Taking your own case to court or tribunal
is for people who do not have a solicitor to represent them in a county
court or magistrates' court or before a tribunal. This book tells you the
procedures to follow in preparing and presenting your case, what happens
at the hearing, what steps can be taken to enforce a judgment, how to
appeal if the judgment goes against you. It explains in layman's terms how
to conduct proceedings yourself in the county court (arbitration for 'small
claims' and open court hearings), in the High Court (rarely appropriate for
a litigant-in-person), in a magistrates' court (for both civil and criminal
matters), at a social security appeal tribunal (challenging a DHSS benefits
decision), before an industrial tribunal (dismissal cases).

Living with stress
helps the reader to identify the sources of stress in his own life – following
a bereavement, in a job or in unemployment, in marriage or before or after
divorce, in loneliness or in overcrowding. It lists the common warning
signs and indicates what steps to take in order to adapt successfully, or
change what needs to be changed.

The book looks at the physical and emotional harm that can result if stress
is not kept under control and unnecessary stress eliminated. It outlines the
right and wrong ways to counteract stress – from smoking, drinking and
drugs to a whole range of beneficial attitudes and activities.

Pregnancy month by month
tells in detail what a pregnant woman can expect at each stage of antenatal
care. The book discusses where to have a baby, and compares hospital, GP
maternity unit, nursing home and home confinement. It gives reasons for
the various tests and examinations at antenatal clinics, and tells how to
deal with the minor ailments that often accompany pregnancy. Sections on
genetic counselling, having twins, claiming maternity benefits, fertility
problems, contraception, abortion and provisions for unmarried mothers
are also included.

The newborn baby
deals primarily with the first weeks after the baby is born, with information about feeding and development in the following weeks and months. The daily routines, such as feeding, bathing, nappy changing, sleeping, are covered and the book tells how to identify and cope with minor upsets that may cause alarm but are normal, and also the more serious ailments that should be reported to the doctor. The book also deals with routine matters such as immunization, tests, visits to the clinic.

Householder's action guide
is for everyone who owns or rents a home. It deals with problems and decisions a householder may have to face, and what action he should take to assert his rights and fulfil his obligations.

Topics include obtaining planning permission (and also how to stop others getting it where their proposal would interfere with your property); the rights and duties of local authority departments towards the householder; rates, and how to appeal against an assessment; legal liability towards visitors, trespassers and casual passers-by; how to deal with nuisance caused by other people; how to avoid disputes with neighbours and, if it is unavoidable, what action to take.

Dealing with household emergencies
aims to help the ordinary, non-too-practical person deal with urgent, relatively straightforward jobs. It offers commonsense advice on how to keep emergencies to a minimum, and gives detailed instructions on how to deal with simple problems.

The contents include: knowing where to turn, electrical emergencies, how to deal with leaks and blockages, fire-preventing and coping, window repairs, quick action for stains, accident first aid, claiming on insurance.

Which? way to buy, sell and move house
takes the strain out of a complicated process by anticipating and answering your questions with detailed advice. Every subject covered is tackled logically and precisely.

Areas covered include: buying first or selling first? getting a mortgage, the cost of moving, looking for a house, making an offer, conveyancing, buying at an auction, selling your house, planning the move, buying and selling in Scotland.

The legal side of buying a house
covers the procedure for buying an owner-occupied house with a registered title in England or Wales (not Scotland). It takes you step by step through a typical house purchase so that, in many cases, you can do your own conveyancing, without a solicitor. It also deals with the legal side of selling.

Other Consumers' Association publications include

Avoiding heart trouble
Which? way to slim
Approaching retirement
What to do when someone dies
A handbook of consumer law
A patients guide to the National Health Service
Renting and letting
The wrong kind of medicine?
The Which? book of insurance
The Which? guide to birth control
A parent's guide to education
Earning money at home
Starting your own business

CA publications are available from Consumers' Association,
Castlemead, Gascoyne Way, Hertford SG14 1LH, and from booksellers.